PEUGEOT 205 T16
Group B Rally Car

1983 to 1988

COVER IMAGE: The late, great Jim Bamber's original cutaway of the 1984 Peugeot 205 Turbo 16.
(Bamber family archive)

First published in December 2020

A catalogue record for this book is available from the British Library.

ISBN 978 1 78521 251 2

Library of Congress control no. 2019934842

Published by J H Haynes & Co. Ltd.,
Sparkford, Yeovil, Somerset BA22 7JJ, UK.
Tel: 01963 440635
Int. tel: +44 1963 440635
Website: www.haynes.com

Haynes North America Inc.,
859 Lawrence Drive, Newbury Park,
California 91320, USA.

Printed in Malaysia.

Senior Commissioning Editor: Steve Rendle
Copy editor: Beth Dymond
Proof reader: Dean Rockett
Indexer: Peter Nicholson
Page design: James Robertson

PEUGEOT 205 T16 Group B Rally Car

1983 to 1988

Enthusiasts' Manual

An insight into the design, engineering and competition history of Peugeot's World Championship-winning rally car

Nick Garton

Contents

OPPOSITE **The Peugeot 205 Turbo 16 in full flight: the only thoroughbred Group B car to win the FIA World Rally Championship.** (*McKlein*)

Introduction

Between 1984 and 1986, the Peugeot 205 Turbo 16 was the most brilliantly successful design to emerge from the short-lived but awe-inspiring Group B era of international rallying. It was an astonishing period for the World Rally Championship, as it was for all forms of motor sport.

The 1980s saw motor sport on a scale that is almost incalculable in today's world, from the cost of developing the cars to the distances covered by each event, staffed by hundreds of people per team and capturing the imagination of millions.

Just look at the films of Group B rallies that we treasure to this day. Not the short clips that are shared on an almost constant loop through social media but rather the full-length coverage of Monte Carlo, the 1000 Lakes, the Safari and the RAC Rally. In each case, the style is uniform, opening with artistic shots of foggy, hazy mornings and spotlights that are accompanied by the best of Jean-Michel Jarre's electronic symphonies – *Equinoxe IV* and *Oxygene II* being particular favourites among the producers of the day.

The story is played out through day and night, through abundant crowds and unpeopled wildernesses, until the victorious crew rolls up onto the ceremonial ramp to claim their laurels and champagne. And the production values are astonishingly high.

For Peugeot, the success of the 205 Turbo 16 was in all likelihood the guarantor of the company's survival. After making several bad investments, having failed to keep pace with modern tastes and with a pensionable product range, the Peugeot-Talbot-Citroën group could very easily have been plunged into a spiral from which there was no escape if it could not make a success of its new 205 supermini – the car on which all of the firm's fortunes were dependent.

Every Peugeot 205 on the road today – whether it's sitting outside student digs in England, carrying out deliveries in Tunisia or pottering through the Côte d'Azur – is now approaching 25 years or more old. The fact that these cars sold so well, so far and wide, and became so cherished was in no small part testament to the success of rallying as a global marketing platform. There may have been precious little carry-over between the road car and the rally car but the image of Ari Vatanen and Juha Kankkunen hurling their 205s through dust, snow and sand created the dynamism and character of the car that saved Peugeot.

BELOW Art and technology combined – small wonder that Jean-Michel Jarre provided the soundtrack to much of the Peugeot 205 Turbo 16's TV coverage.
(Alamy)

LEFT Peugeot's survival into the 1990s depended upon the success of rallying to sell its chic little hatchback, many of which remain cherished today, almost 25 years after they went out of production. *(Alamy)*

Acknowledgements

Sincere thanks are due to many people who helped make this book happen, not least Steve Rendle at Haynes Publishing for commissioning it and for his infinite patience while it was being delivered. Also to my wife and family for their patience while living with a bloke who has a head full of old competition cars and is prone to missing mealtimes.

Reinhard Klein deserves a standing ovation for his part, not only in allowing me the run of his unique archive of images but also through the Slowly Sideways movement and his dedication to maintaining opportunities for new generations to share the enjoyment of witnessing these cars in action. Also thanks to Lucy Bamber and the Bamber family for allowing us to use the late, great Jim Bamber's timeless cutaway artwork.

To the brilliant Ari Vatanen and Juha Kankkunen, to Jean-Pierre Nicolas, Michèle Mouton, Carlos Barros, Timo Salonen, Mick Linford, Paul White, Richard Rodgers, Mark Donaldson, Kari Mäkelä, Jonathan Gill, Ben Buesnel, James Crofts, the team at Bonhams, the organisers at Race Retro and to Tim Foster and all at Rallying with Group B, my

enormous thanks for your support and time.

Thank you to Andy Bye at the Rootes Trust Archive Centre, who came galloping to the rescue in the middle of his Christmas holiday. I'm also deeply indebted to the support of experts in forums such as Caradisiac, to Mick Wood of the best of the Peugeot 205 Turbo 16 groups on Facebook, to Sylvain Chavey and many more – with apologies for my schoolboy French. Also to Gareth Jex and Phil Field for their Slot Rally insights.

To all at Peugeot UK and the Coventry Transport Museum, to Peugeot's head office and its team at the Schlumpf Museum, again most profound thanks for all the contributions, great or small, to the finished product.

This book completes a 'turbo trilogy' alongside my previous Haynes Manuals on the great competition cars of the 1980s, alongside the Audi Quattro and the Porsche 956/962. It also touches on the Ferrari 312T and the Royal Aircraft Factory S.E.5 for which I have also written Haynes books – it's a small world, even across several decades!

This book is dedicated to my eldest daughters, Electra and Tallulah.

Chapter One

The Peugeot 205 Turbo 16 story

The Group B era of rallying lasted from 1982 to 1986 and was dominated by two cars: the production-based Audi Quattro, which had already revolutionised the sport with four-wheel-drive and turbo power, and the Peugeot 205 Turbo 16, which took the technical creativity of Group B to its limits. There were many equally exotic Group B rally cars of seemingly limitless potential to appear in this brief window of time, but none could match the performance, results or sheer importance of the car with which Peugeot fought back to financial health: the remarkable 'Turbo Seize...'.

OPPOSITE **The Peugeot 205 Turbo 16 was the product of decades of evolution in the sport twinned with its parent manufacturer's proud history.** *(McKlein)*

9

Rallying: From gentlemen to players

American NASCAR legend 'The King' Richard Petty once posited: 'There is no doubt about precisely when folks began racing each other in automobiles. It was the day they built the second automobile.' While nobody should ever doubt The King's word on this, the first official motor races (starting with the 1894 Paris–Lyon marathon) could very easily be described as rallies; cars competing on the open road from point-to-point, rather than circulating around a track.

It was in the glittering haven of Monte Carlo that the sport really took shape, however. In 1909 the Sport Automobile Vélocipédique Monégasque motor club began to plan an event to draw the great and the good to the principality in their motor cars, in order to spend lots of money when they got there. The idea, attributed to Prince Albert I, was for cars to start from various cities around Europe and, after much hardship and derring-do, arrive on the Côte d'Azur in good order with their wallets at the ready.

In January 1911, 23 cars set out from 11 different locations and the first man to arrive was Henri Rougier, who had driven 634 miles (1,020km) from Paris on a 25hp Turcat-Méry. When the rest of the field arrived, the Monégasques held a *concours d'élégance* to appraise the competing cars on their elegance, comfort and general condition – after which Rougier was declared the overall winner.

The Monte Carlo Rally rapidly became established on the social calendar very quickly, while the sport of rallying really took off after World War One, when cars were more abundant – as well as faster and more reliable. The vastly depleted generation of young European men who survived the war went in search of thrills, and motor sport in all its forms became a terrific outlet. Among the many events to spring up in the 1920s and 1930s, the International Alpine Trial covered much of the south of France, Switzerland and Austria. Many adventurous young Britons took part – including future grand prix winner Dick Seaman and 007 creator Ian Fleming. In Britain, the Royal Automobile Club established an all-British event in 1932, when 341 competitors in unmodified cars started from nine different towns and cities (London, Bath, Norwich, Leamington, Buxton, Harrogate, Liverpool, Newcastle upon Tyne and Edinburgh), each with 1,000 miles (1,600km) to cover before converging in Torquay.

Another explosion of interest in rallying followed World War Two, and most of the world's great rallies were founded during the course of the 1950s: the Coronation Rally in Kenya (later the Safari Rally), the 1000 Lakes in Finland and the Acropolis Rally in Greece. Motor manufacturers began to invest huge prestige in rallying success, all the more so with the advent of timed 'special stages' to add a truly competitive edge to the events. Works rally teams appeared, usually integral to the factories in which the customer cars were built, and a new generation of specialised team managers like Stuart Turner at the British Motor Corporation worked over every detail of the sport's rules and regulations to take advantage of every loophole.

This was the period in which rallying changed from being an enjoyable caper for well-heeled gentlemen like Ian Fleming to a hard-nosed professional sport in which the

RIGHT Although the first motor races can equally be described as the start of rallying, the first event to give the sport its name was the inaugural Monte Carlo Rally of 1911. *(ACM)*

RIGHT Rallying was the inspiration for many of the adventures undertaken by fictional hero James Bond. The creator of agent 007, Ian Fleming, had come to know the thrill of racing through the Alps in a sports car during the 1930s. *(Getty Images)*

players were very serious about their business. As one example of Turner's brilliance, he fielded Mini-Coopers whose engines covered an array of sizes – from 970cc to 1,275cc and all points in between – often on the same event. No loophole was too small to be valuable in keeping the Mini firmly in place as the star car of the sixties until eventually the sport's governing body, the Fédération Internationale de l'Automobile (FIA), had to do something to manage the chaos and new technical regulations were implemented.

Group 1 was for standard production cars of which no fewer than 5,000 per year should be made. Group 2, 'improved touring cars', required a minimum 1,000 production examples, as did Group 3 for production sports cars. As the decade came to a close, most manufacturers were focused upon a new generation of Group 4 'special grand touring cars', of which only 500 examples were required to be built, and it was

these cars that launched the FIA World Rally Championship in 1973.

It began as a title for manufacturers, in part to reward them for their commitment to the series and also to help prevent the marquee teams from cherry-picking only the biggest events on the calendar. Ford developed Group 4 versions of its humdrum Escort at colossal expense, the Mk.I RS1600 and later the Mk. II RS1800, and other recognisable showroom cars included the handsome Peugeot 504

BELOW The British Motor Corporation team under Stuart Turner exploited every opportunity to win the greatest of rallies with the tiniest of cars – the Mini-Cooper S. *(McKlein)*

ABOVE **The Lancia Stratos electrified Group 4 rallying in the 1970s: a bespoke competition car from the ground up built purely for competitive use. Crowds loved it, but competitors were forced to spend more to keep up.** *(McKlein/Vessely)*

coupé, Citroën's venerable DS limousine and the Saab 99. Fiat had its slinkier 124 coupé, then Renault had its specialist-built Alpine A110 coupé and the Porsche 911 proved to be a formidable rally car in all conditions.

As the seventies progressed, ever-more exotic machinery was built to Group 4 regulations, of which the real game changer was the Lancia Stratos. This was a design concept built for wowing the crowds at the 1971 Turin Motor Show: beautiful and futuristic but hopelessly impractical. This

car was evolved into a Ferrari-engined rally thoroughbred that cast aside any pretence of a relationship with the type of cars to be found in a local dealership – and it dominated the mid-seventies.

Although the Stratos forced rival manufacturers to invest huge sums in competing against it with production-based models like the Ford Escort and Opel Ascona, an increasing number of car brands could be found seeking a share of the limelight that rallying enjoyed. One such was the relatively insignificant brand, Audi, which had been under numerous owners since the 1930s until it was finally bought by Volkswagen in 1966.

Under the stewardship of Ferdinand Porsche's grandson, Ferdinand Piëch, the company had been quietly engineering high-quality cars built around a five-cylinder engine design. Piëch and his engineers were always out to find innovative ideas, and after winning the Paris–Dakar marathon with a Volkswagen Iltis jeep, they lobbied the FIA to allow four-wheel-drive systems in rallying.

The Germans' case was made much easier because nobody at that time believed that a four-wheel-drive car would work: received wisdom declared that such a transmission would be too heavy and too complex to survive the sport's rigours... but in 1981 the Audi Quattro appeared and rewrote the parameters of rally car performance.

At the time, when the Fédération Internationale du Sport Automobile (FISA) granted Audi's wish of entering the sport with four-wheel-drive, it was prescribing an entirely new structure to all of its production-based categories, including rallying, touring car racing and sports cars. Out went Groups 1–4 and in came Groups A, B and C.

The primary agitator for change and simplification of the classes was the recently elected head of the FIA's sporting division, FISA. Jean-Marie Balestre was a journalist and publisher with a flair for showbiz (see Chapter 5), and he wanted to see his sport grow and flourish across all of its disciplines. This meant accessible, easily understood categories that brought exciting competition and grabbed headlines around the world.

Group A was for 'modified touring cars',

BELOW **Group A became the principal production-based class for touring cars and rallying. It was pressed into a lead role at the end of the Group B era and in most respects remains the basis of modern WRC regulations.** *(McKlein)*

which meant that no fewer than 5,000 standard production examples of the competing car had to be made in the preceding year (later reduced to 2,500), and 25,000 of the volume model upon which it was based – for example, the Ford Sierra Cosworth and the humble Ford Sierra in all its many forms.

Group B was an almost wide-open formula for any car with a minimum of two seats that effectively replaced both Group 4 (modified) and Group 5 (silhouette) classes for touring car and GT racing and the top class of rallying. In theory, it meant that a car like the Lancia Stratos could compete against a Porsche or a Ferrari and that other manufacturers could build equally exotic cars.

With a minimum production run of 200 examples in total, the manufacturers could then build 20 competition cars – or evolutions – of the original. Further evolutions would be permitted every 12 months, but it was felt that the major manufacturers would actually spend less to build a relative handful of bespoke cars than they spent building high-specification versions of production models.

Completing the set, Group C was designed to replace the old Group 5 silhouette cars and the Group 6 sports prototypes, as two-seat sports cars to go endurance racing. No minimum production run of chassis would be needed and beyond the dimensions and fuel consumption, everything else was left to the manufacturers to sort out.

In each case, these new groups and their specific regulations were designed to come into force at the start of 1982 and remain stable for a minimum of five years (i.e. to the start of 1987). This promised stability did indeed convince motor manufacturers that some spending would be repaid if they could get five years' worth of competition out of it – and the resulting level of competition and entertainment across the motor sport world was a ringing endorsement of Balestre's original vision.

Touring car racing, rallying and Le Mans-style endurance racing all enjoyed a huge groundswell of media and public interest. This, in turn, brought lavish commercial sponsorship, which in turn paid for huge promotional and marketing campaigns that reached more media and public. It was a self-

perpetuating cycle in which Group B rallying was to play a vital role.

While FISA was thrashing out the final rules for its new class structure, Audi stole a march on the competition through the dying days of Group 4 rallying. In its first year the Audi Quattro was indeed overweight and unreliable, as had been predicted by the naysayers... but on loose surfaces none of the traditional cars stood a chance, and every retirement meant that a lesson was being learnt by the Audi engineers through the 1981 season.

ABOVE The Porsche 911 was able to transition from Group 4 to Group B with very little modification, which was largely the intention of the rules when written. FISA never expected that it would be left trailing by four-wheel-drive turbo cars. *(McKlein)*

BELOW Porsche's 962 was the most abundant model used in Group C racing, sold from the factory to privateer teams and competing against Lancia, Jaguar, Mercedes-Benz, Aston Martin, Toyota, Nissan, Mazda and others. *(Author)*

ABOVE The Group 4 Audi Quattro suffered numerous teething problems but ultimately came to dominate the twilight period before Group B got into its stride. The evidence that turbocharging and four-wheel-drive were the way of the future in Group B was overwhelming. *(Author)*

RIGHT Armand Peugeot led the family business into bicycle production and then the nascent automotive industry. *(Alamy)*

In 1982, Group B regulations came into force – albeit with very few cars. As a concession halfway through the year, FISA allowed Group 4 cars to be considered to be Group B, provided that the manufacturers could provide evidence that they were working up a full Group B car. Lancia was first out of the blocks with its winsome little 037 Rallye, which appeared late in the 1982 season. Ostensibly based upon the Beta Montecarlo coupé, the 037 was a bespoke supercharged rear-drive design that owed much to its predecessor, the Stratos. Doubtless, FISA was delighted.

Elsewhere, Ford was preparing a Group B version of its new front-wheel-drive Escort and the rules allowed Porsches and Ferraris to compete alongside these purpose-built cars. But as the countdown towards the Group B era quickened, there came word of a new operation being put together in France: there would be a Group B car from Peugeot. Some spoke of it being mid-engined, like the Lancia, and four-wheel-drive like a Quattro – but nobody thought that was achievable, still less by a very conservative firm like Peugeot.

The industrious Peugeots and 'les Charlatans'

The Peugeot family of the Doubs region in France were established as flour millers, dyers and tanners until 1810, when the brothers Jean-Frederic and Jean-Pierre Peugeot established a foundry in the mill and began producing sprung steel. An array of Peugeot steel products began to emerge, from watch mechanisms to coffee grinders and, in 1858, Jean-Pierre Peugeot's son Émile applied for the use of a lion as the company logo.

Émile's son Armand was keen to expand the family business much further, and a visit to England's industrial Midlands in 1881 convinced him to invest in bicycle manufacturing. As with so many English bicycle factories, the move towards motoring was not far behind, with Peugeot displaying an experimental steam-powered tricycle at the 1889 World's Fair. The arrival of internal combustion engines convinced Armand Peugeot to enter the nascent motor car market, setting up an offshoot company with his cousin Eugène Peugeot in 1892, called Les Fils de Peugeot Frères, using a licence bought from the Daimler company in Germany.

Armand Peugeot wanted to increase capacity and make the production of cars and trucks their primary business, but Eugène refused to commit. This led Armand to found the Société Anonyme des Automobiles Peugeot in 1896 and build a new factory at Audincourt, which would become the largest motor manufacturer in France – reaching 10,000 cars per year by 1910.

From the outset, Peugeot had used competition as a means to promote its products and in 1894 a 3hp Peugeot Type 7 driven by Albert Lemaître was classified as the winner of what is recognised as the world's first official motor race from Paris to Rouen. Meanwhile, Eugène Peugeot had also continued to build cars through Les Fils de Peugeot Frères, under the Lion-Peugeot brand name.

There was no reconciliation between the two cousins but, with the death of Eugène Peugeot in 1907, Armand Peugeot was brought back into the fold. With no heir to his own business, Armand agreed to merge his company with the rest of the Peugeot family interests in 1910 in return for one million francs per year.

This put Eugène Peugeot's three sons in charge of the entire Peugeot business, of whom Robert Peugeot was the most proactive. Robert Peugeot's chauffeur was an aspiring racing driver by the name of Jules Goux, who would take the wheel of a succession of purposeful Peugeots for Voiturette ('light car') racing. The success of Goux, alongside

teammates Giosuè Guippone and the swashbuckling Georges Boillot, encouraged Robert Peugeot to take the firm into the new and high-stakes world of grand prix racing, and to do so by procuring the talents of designer Ernest Henry and driver Paolo Zuccarelli from Peugeot's great rivals at Hispano-Suiza.

A new Peugeot racing department was established in the Parisian suburb of Suresnes. Today this team led by Henry, Zuccarelli,

ABOVE This is the third Peugeot engine built under licence from Daimler, the 188th of its kind, with a manufacturing date of 1890. This single-cylinder unit was recently discovered intact and is under restoration at the Coventry Transport Museum. *(Author)*

LEFT Albert Lemaître won what is now regarded as the first official motor race, the 1894 Paris-Lyon, on a 3hp Peugeot. Here he sits in the winning car alongside tyre manufacturer, Adolphe Clément-Bayard. *(Peugeot)*

Boillot and Goux is known as 'les Charlatans', although the origins of the name are disputed to this day. Some say that the Peugeot workforce named the team as Charlatans because they did not work out of one of the main factories, and because many of the more specialised car parts had to be fabricated by specialists from outside Peugeot.

There is another explanation that suggests that Zuccarelli arrived in Paris with the details of Hispano-Suiza designer Marc Birkigt's groundbreaking 'Monobloc' engine, cast from a single piece of metal either on paper or with enough knowledge to relay the fundamental principles to the designer Henry so that he could build his own version.

The result was a series of remarkable engines with a 'Monobloc' construction, dual overhead camshafts and four valves per cylinder in 'v' formation that were the mirror image of one of Birkigt's Hispano-Suiza engines. After debuting with promise in national races during 1911, Georges Boillot took a famous victory for 'les Charlatans' with victory at the 1912 Grand Prix. This success led Goux to claim the 1913 Indianapolis 500 – the first time that a foreign manufacturer had claimed the great American race – while

French joy redoubled when Boillot retained the grand prix winner's laurels in the same year.

Europe stood on the precipice in 1914, when Boillot's Peugeot was eventually worn down by a concerted team effort from Mercedes to deliver a famous victory for Germany just a few weeks before the outbreak of World War One. During the war, Boillot found new fame as a fighter pilot until his death in action in 1916. After the war, Boillot's brother André drove the L45 to victory in the 1919 Targa Florio.

The brief, bright years in which 'les Charlatans' triumphed were bittersweet indeed. They brought enormous success to Peugeot at some cost to its reputation, and in so doing established new benchmarks for a manufacturer's competition team. Marc Birkigt and Hispano-Suiza meanwhile went on to develop the astonishing V8 Monobloc aircraft engine, which powered the finest allied fighters of the war such as the French SPAD and British S.E.5, sleek machines made famous by aces including Georges Guynemer, Eddie Rickenbacker and Albert Ball... many of which had engines made by the Peugeot factories as part of their contribution to the war effort.

During the 1920s, Peugeot split its

BELOW Peugeot's specialist team of drivers and engineers set up shop in Paris and gloried in the nickname 'les Charlatans' to dominate motor sport's biggest events in Europe and America. Here the charismatic Georges Boillot sits in the first of Peugeot's successful line of grand prix cars in 1912.
(Getty Images)

bicycle and motorcycle business away from its car and truck operation to form Cycles Peugeot. The car business continued to thrive, swallowing rivals such as De Dion and Bellanger, but suffered severely during World War Two. Many of the Peugeot workforce were seized by the occupying German forces and transferred back to the Fatherland to work as effective slave labour for the engineering projects being managed by Ferdinand Porsche. It was for this crime against the Peugeot workforce that Porsche was eventually arrested and jailed soon after the end of hostilities, after Peugeot had repatriated its surviving workers and their equipment on a train proudly swathed in *le Tricolore*.

The sleek American-style Peugeot 203 became its first post-war flagship model, beating the likes of BMW and Jaguar to win the 1950 Liège–Rome–Liège rally. As the French economy recovered, and successive governments increased public spending and reduced working hours, so the passion for car ownership increased among French households. French car ownership rocketed from 1.7 million vehicles in 1950 to 14 million in 1973 – and Peugeot was by far the most popular provider of inexpensive, rugged and durable cars for national tastes.

What the French motor industry did not anticipate, however, was the increased competition brought about by the European

ABOVE The Hispano-Suiza V8 engine was the World War One equivalent of the Rolls-Royce Merlin and powered the best air-to-air fighting machines of the war, such as the French SPAD and the British S.E.5 (pictured). Many features of the design were common with Peugeot's racing engines... the question of who got there first is unresolved. *(Author)*

BELOW Peugeot became the leading domestic motor manufacturer with the exotic American-influenced 203 competing in rallies while its humbler stablemates became volume sellers prized for rugged, user-friendly transport. *(McKlein)*

Common Market. Not only were the manufacturers now paying more for their employees to work less, but they were also confronted by the mighty German motor industry with no tax barrier between them.

French cars may have been cheerful, chic and rugged but they could offer little resistance to the appeal of a granite-hewn Mercedes or no-nonsense VW. Consolidation became the only answer, and Peugeot bought a 30% share of struggling Citroën in 1974, then took over completely in 1975 after the French government gave a large dowry to help create the PSA Group. PSA then bought the European arm of Chrysler in 1978 and rebranded its models as Talbots.

The Chrysler brands of Matra and Talbot brought with them some potentially exciting designs, like the well-thought-out Sunbeam hatchback, but also ancient and decrepit factories that were beset with industrial relations issues. The election of socialist leader François Mitterrand to the French presidency in 1981 only compounded Peugeot's discomfort. Policies aimed at stimulating consumption, further cutting work hours and increasing paid holiday entitlements, threatened to tip PSA over the brink.

Peugeot's president was a former sales manager called Jean Boillot (who was not related to either Georges or André Boillot, despite common misconceptions). In

confronting what was, by any stretch of the imagination, a hazardous outlook for PSA, he pushed through the changes that he believed would give Peugeot and its increasingly unwelcome siblings Citroën and Talbot the best chance of survival.

A major motor sport campaign was planned to promote the group's products, and in 1979 this job fell to Claude Charavay, a former regional sales manager for Peugeot who had been named as head of the competitions programme with little real knowledge of the sport.

Charavet decided that the future lay in buying a stake in Guy Ligier's Formula 1 team and supplying it with an update of the Matra V12 engines that had powered three consecutive Le Mans wins in the early 1970s. The Matra V12 had also seen some success in Formula 1 earlier in the decade, and the idea of bright blue cars racing *pour la gloire de la France* seemed like a very good idea.

PSA decided to use Talbot, formerly Chrysler Europe, as the brand for motor sport and this high-profile partnership enjoyed a bright start to the 1981 season, with team leader Jacques Laffite making the early running in the points race. This pace flattered to deceive, however, and it soon became clear that the writing was on the wall for a big V12 engine like the Matra when smaller turbo engines gave more power and, crucially, more space for aerodynamic innovation.

A plan was then hatched for PSA to buy a supply of BMW turbo engines but this deal collapsed and Ligier was forced to continue with the old V12, which contributed to the departure of the team's esteemed technical chief Gérard Ducarouge. The promise that had been shown in early 1981 faded and by 1982 the team was a lame duck.

Beneath Charavay, a large number of well-informed motor sport folk had been stamping their feet in frustration as they saw good money being thrown after bad. While the Ligier programme was stumbling backwards through one disaster to the next, the humbler Talbot rally operation was poised to win the 1981 World Rally Championship for Manufacturers with its rorty little Sunbeam Lotus.

This was a sport that Peugeot knew well, thanks to the virtues of rugged construction,

BELOW Rugged simplicity wore thin as a selling point when the Common Market allowed French car buyers the opportunity to buy Volkswagen Golfs without huge tariffs. The Germans went on the offensive and cars like the Peugeot 104 could not compete. (Peugeot)

and had come to dominate the marquee events in Africa as well as showing strongly on other events over the years. To a man, those who knew about motor sport at PSA could see that no good was going to come of its Formula 1 dalliance as the company drifted ever-closer towards the rocks. Within this group, the belief grew that PSA needed to cut its losses, but they needed to identify the right replacement for Formula 1 to present to the management. It just so happened that the ideal car upon which to base their programme was entering the final stages of development.

M24: the great white hope

The plans for Peugeot's first design aimed at a truly international marketplace had been laid in 1977–78 and given the codename M24. This would be the Common Market-buster: PSA's rival to increasingly affordable German technology that would pitch unmistakably French design flair, durability and sheer *joie de vivre* against the superior fit and finish for which the likes of the Volkswagen Golf were becoming known.

The initial specification for M24 was undeniably a challenge for even the most audacious designer. It included cost-conscious

considerations such as being lighter and more fuel-efficient than the existing Peugeot 104. It had to be as easy and cheap to build as the outgoing car and utilise as many existing parts as possible to enable Peugeot to save money on research and development. All of this made commercial sense, but it did not sound particularly sexy as a marketing pitch and neither did it inspire much hope in terms of build quality.

ABOVE Gérard Welter was a Peugeot designer during the week but designed and built his own sports prototypes to compete in the Le Mans 24 Hours: here the WM-Peugeot 79/80 shared by rally star Guy Fréquelin and Roger Dorchy takes part in the 1980 Le Mans 24 Hours. *(Motorsport Images)*

Boillot envisaged an entirely new car, designed to appeal to young buyers around the world, so when styling house Pininfarina turned out a design that looked like an enlarged Peugeot 104, it proved to be something of a disappointment. In a moment of inspiration, in-house designer Gérard Welter was called upon to invest the M24 project with some home-grown flair. He was more than up to the job.

Although he had been a Peugeot employee from the age of 17, Welter had a passion for motor sport that led him to build his own cars to compete in the Le Mans 24 Hours. This obsession was tolerated by Welter's superiors – indeed, some parts for his racing cars were fabricated on Peugeot's equipment, and he usually powered them with the company's engines – thanks largely to the quality of work that he delivered for the company.

Many of the most inspired elements of Peugeot's designs over the previous 20 years had originated from Welter, including the celebrated headlight design shared by the Peugeot 304 and 504, which Welter attributed to his infatuation with Sofia Loren's eyes.

Under Boillot's close attention, Welter transformed the Pininfarina design simply by taking the spare wheel from its traditional position in the engine bay (a carry-over from the old Peugeot 104), and shoving it under the boot. This dropped the bonnet line

LEFT Welter's iconic headlights graced models such as the 304 Cabriolet in the 1960s and 1970s. Jules Boillot sought him out to rescue the M24 when Pininfarina underdelivered. *(Peugeot)*

significantly, giving the little car a rakish new look. Welter and his team then smoothed out the car's angular lines for a more modern, curved shape.

'It was a mixture of tradition, elegance and dynamism', recalled Dominique de Guibert, head of Peugeot testing in the 1980s. 'Each month, [Boillot] came to spend an afternoon at Belchamps on the Peugeot test track. I made him try the cars. When he climbed in, he touched the materials and when he drove, he loved the speed and he listened to the car.'

The finishing touch was to be the M24's name – initially it was planned to be 105, the natural successor to the 104, but Boillot personally intervened and declared that this car needed to offer more. This would be a new car of a new class, a revival of the successes of the 202 and 203 in the early post-war era. As a result, the new model would be called the Peugeot 205.

As the production car was being tested to destruction by the road car development team, Boillot's attention began to turn towards how he was going to market the vehicle. Rallying would be perfect, but he needed someone with experience in the sport that Claude Charavay lacked to bring the project together. As it happened, many of Boillot's lieutenants agreed that there was one man who would fit the bill perfectly, and his name was Jean Todt.

The king is dead: long live the king

While Charavay had stumbled from one disaster to the next, Jean Todt had already begun his rise towards succession. He was merely a co-driver, a freelance member of Des O'Dell's Talbot team who had, over the preceding dozen years, built a career by guiding many of the sport's biggest stars to success with his unflappable presence in the car and bulletproof management of every detail of each event.

ABOVE Pininfarina's initial sculpture of the Peugeot M24 was a mildly reworked offering of the marque's 1970s models. Jules Boillot was uninspired by it, and sought a more modern design that would win over younger buyers. *(Peugeot)*

LEFT Gérard Welter (third from left) and his team show Jules Boillot (centre) around their reworked mock-up of M24. Already the basic shape of the Peugeot 205 is clear to see – soon it would become familiar to millions of rally fans and prospective buyers. *(Peugeot)*

Not only was Todt a brilliant co-driver, but also he was a shrewd reader of men. He gathered a loyal core of followers around him; including O'Dell, the team's leading driver Guy Fréquelin, Peugeot PR-man-cum-journalist Olivier Quesnel and the then-current head of PR at Peugeot, Corrado Provera.

As if by magic, during 1980–81, a number of unfavourable stories began to appear in the French motoring press about Peugeot in motor sport, and Charavay in particular. While Peugeot's management pored over these stories over their *petit déjeuner*, Provera and Fréquelin lobbied internally at PSA for Boillot to

meet with Todt and hear his opinions – which Boillot agreed to in June 1981.

Not only did Todt present a forthright and damning account of Charavay's management of PSA's competition programmes, but he also presented a vision of the future in which rallying – with all its benefits of road relevance and customer interaction – would be at the forefront. New regulations to govern the sport – FISA's Group B – would allow greater technological freedom, and thereby allow Peugeot to harness all of the expertise within its considerable empire towards building an unbeatable new car.

Boillot listened and said that he would get in touch. This he did two months later, when he invited Todt to a meeting with Peugeot's general manager, Lucien Collaine. By this time, Todt had gained the ear of none other than Jean-Philippe Peugeot, who had given him some insights into the M24 programme. As a result of this, Todt went in to the meeting with all guns blazing: his vision being one of an M24 rally car to dominate the new Group B rally formula.

One thing upon which Todt insisted was that the M24 rally programme should be launched at exactly the same time as the road car. The two designs should be bonded together in the public eye so that anyone buying a humble little 954cc base model 205 felt that they were getting a little bit of the magic and glamour from the rally programme. This was music to the ears of a sales impresario like Jean Boillot.

Both Boillot and Collaine were impressed by the sheer force of will that confronted them in the ambitious Todt; the corporate-mindedness of his plan and, no doubt, the assiduousness with which this mere rally co-driver had pieced together the requisite contacts and knowledge from within Peugeot's hierarchy. More meetings followed – with the research and development team at Garenne-Colombes, and in Paris with PSA's commercial director and with the head of personnel.

Like a whirlwind, Todt went through the entire M24 programme and virtually every major office of PSA in the space of less than two months. This sprint through the halls and corridors ended with the golden ticket that Todt had so longed for: a contract to become the manager of Peugeot's competitions department. Claude Charavay was history, and so too was the Ligier deal. In 1983, PSA would focus all of its energies upon the M24.

This seismic shift took place while Todt was still on duty as a co-driver with the Peugeot and Talbot works teams. Even after signing his contract to take command, Todt competed in one last event from the passenger seat of Guy Fréquelin's Sunbeam Lotus: the 1981 RAC Rally, in which they crashed out on the second day. The accident plucked the drivers' championship from Fréquelin's hands and placed them into those of Finnish superstar Ari Vatanen – Ford's first and only drivers' title until 2017 – but Talbot was still the manufacturers' champion.

Jean Todt shut the door and stepped away from the car with no regrets. 'I have never believed in symbols and souvenirs', he said. 'The future alone interests me. Another life began.'

Les nouveaux Charlatans

At a press conference that marked one of his first official duties, Jean Todt described his timetable to bring the World Rally Championship titles to Peugeot. A new car would be built to full Group B specifications and a testing programme would take place through 1983. The car would be homologated on 1 April 1984, then its testing programme would be competed by entering a limited number of events through the year as a prelude to delivering the world championship in 1985.

A good proportion of Todt's audience scoffed at the audacity of a man in his first managerial role making victory sound assured. Audi had gone rallying with the full might of Volkswagen's chequebook behind it and the leadership of Porsche scion Ferdinand Piëch, the architect of Porsche's Le Mans success, at its head... and yet Audi Sport had spent an awful lot of the 1981 season watching its Quattros catch fire.

It is not thought that Todt shared their hesitancy even for a second. He got straight on with the business of being the boss. The first job was to create a new base of operations for the team, and for him that could only mean Paris. Yes, Des O'Dell was running a world-class operation from the Peugeot-owned workshop in Coventry but Todt would need to be nearer to the corridors of power in PSA, and that meant the French capital.

The property he chose was on the Rue Paul Bert in Boulogne-Billancourt, five miles west of the city centre. Whether the echoes of *les Charlatans* setting up shop in Paris 70 years earlier held any resonance to Todt is unlikely, but the parallels are obvious, not least that he then moved swiftly to close down Peugeot's existing competitions departments in the factories at Sochaux and La Garenne – particularly in the latter case, which remained the main centre for Peugeot's research and development work.

To help offset the discord of his actions, Todt gathered up several key players from the existing motor sport operation and gave

LEFT Todt established a new department with its headquarters in Paris, closing down the Peugeot race and rally operations in Sochaux and La Garenne.
(Peugeot)

them key roles within the new project team in Paris. What he left firmly in the old workshops, however, was the prototype Group B car that had been assembled by his predecessors: a Peugeot 305 saloon that had been fitted with the V6 engine and rear-wheel-drive from Peugeot's proven 505, a few lightweight panels and a modest rear spoiler. Todt was no engineer, but he knew enough to see how dismal the car's prospects would be.

Not one element of the 305 project would make the grade for Todt's proposed 'M24 Rallye', as it was known internally. One man whom Todt trusted, and who had supported his rise to the big job, was Talbot's proven rally man Des O'Dell, and so he took up Todt's invitation to work in Paris on the new wonder-car. While his new team grappled with a clean sheet of paper, Todt meanwhile ensured that his offices were fitted out with all the latest mod cons, including a telecom, to provide the requisite level of gravitas and sophistication.

With the look and feel of his premises thus in place, Todt then set about the look and feel of his new operation. One element would be the name, which needed to give primacy to Peugeot while having resonance throughout the PSA Group. After a process of elimination he settled upon Peugeot Talbot Sport, which was swiftly passed by the top brass within PSA. Having got a name, Todt then took an active role in creating the brand identity for his new outfit – drawing less upon the lion and more upon the sort of logos that were appearing in the fashion industry.

'The logo would have to include the deep blue and yellow colours of Peugeot, and the light blue of Talbot', Todt later recalled. 'I wanted to add red to signify the dynamic nature of rallying. Jeff Davis, a designer from the Peugeot graphics department at Poissy, made several sketches. We chose one that was rather forceful, and that promoted the department from its rally car to its stationery.'

Everyone agreed that the M24 Rallye should be mid-engined and four-wheel-drive. The question of which engine should be employed proved to be a thorny one, with Todt insisting that it should be a turbo rather than a large capacity V6. Turbo engines, his engineers reasoned, were rather more complex, prone

to throttle lag and, as anyone who tuned in regularly to Formula 1's growing TV coverage knew, prone to pulling off at the side of the track with a huge white cumulonimbus of mechanical failure stretching out behind them.

Eventually, the engineers collectively produced their definitive plan for the layout of the M24 Rallye. It would feature the new XU four-cylinder petrol and diesel engine, which would be the mainstay of the 205 range of road cars, mounted transversely on the right-hand side of the car, with a gearbox taken from the PSA parts bin on the left-hand side of the car and a turbocharger behind them.

It was a neat and tidy way of packaging the car to fit within the tiny confines of the M24 road car's bodyshell, even when stretched to the maximum proportions permissible in the regulations. It also brought with it some issues of stability, and added complications in the design and manufacture of the 200 road cars that would need to be built to the same standards as every other road car.

The details of what they designed and how will be covered in Chapter 4, but in the space of 14 months from a standing start, the new team was in place on the eve of the 1983 Geneva Motor Show, standing around a gleaming white rally car that proudly wore the new multi-colour 'swoosh' of Peugeot Talbot Sport. From the outset, the 205 Turbo 16 and the 205 road car were inseparable in the public gaze, in press materials, in motor shows and in advertisements. Yes, the rally car was fractionally different in its proportions but there was no mistaking what it was: a new Peugeot 205.

It would take another 14 months to hone it for its debut on the World Rally Championship trail, but this was still a landmark achievement for Todt and his team, one worthy of celebration to have achieved what had often seemed like an impossible mission to launch the road and rally cars together. Throughout 1983, Jean-Pierre Nicolas and the engineers got to work on their gruelling programme of testing while Todt kept an iron fist on the budgets, the paperwork, and the politics with the FIA, FISA and the other manufacturers. His other concern was finding the right driver to

lead them out onto the field: a truly top-flight star capable of getting the car to victory as quickly as possible.

Initially, Todt was satisfied that he had already got his man, in the form of Stig Blomqvist. The Swede, who had made his name hustling front-wheel-drive Saabs around with aplomb, had become generally recognised as the greatest all-rounder in rallying since the Trollhättan marque had withdrawn from the world championship.

Blomqvist had signed his contract with Des O'Dell's team in late 1981, when his third place on the RAC Rally had secured Talbot its manufacturers' world championship title. The Talbot programme would be reduced for 1982 in order to ensure primacy of the M24 Rallye project, and so Blomqvist had done another deal to drive for Audi's Swedish importer in national competitions. With a full works-specification Quattro at his disposal, the Swede's eyes had been opened to the potential of four-wheel-drive turbocharged rally cars, and he wasn't prepared to wait for Todt's brand-new

ABOVE Wearing Jean Todt's new corporate colours and driving Des O'Dell's Talbot Sunbeam Lotus at the 1982 RAC Rally, Stig Blomqvist seemed the ideal man to lead Peugeot Talbot Sport into battle. *(McKlein)*

BELOW Blomqvist chose to jump ship to Audi in 1983, where he would become recognised as the fastest of the team's drivers and would claim the 1984 world championship. This left Jean Todt looking for a new star to lead the team. *(McKlein)*

team to create an unproven prototype when Audi already had a world-beater.

Blomqvist decided to switch allegiance to Audi's world championship squad, where he proved to be easily the fastest and most spectacular of the Quattro drivers – although he would not get a chance to capitalise on his status until 1984. The team's anchor in the driving line-up was Finnish veteran Hannu Mikkola, and he had been promised absolute primacy in his bid for the 1983 drivers' title – terms to which Blomqvist agreed.

Todt was stung deeply by the rejection, and drew up a shortlist of candidates to fill the seat that Blomqvist had vacated. His first port of call was double world champion Walter Röhrl, who had beaten Audi's Michèle Mouton to the 1982 drivers' title in an antiquated Opel

and was, in 1983, helping Lancia to deny Audi the manufacturers' title through sheer force of will.

Röhrl looked seriously at Todt's offer but in the end he signed a contract with Audi for 1984, primarily for the opportunity to measure himself against Blomqvist in the same car. Audi was so overjoyed at the prospect of having Röhrl in its camp rather than having to compete against him that it agreed to almost all of the Bavarian's unique demands, such as picking his own selection of events to compete in based on how much he enjoyed them and not having to do any PR work for the team sponsor, a tobacco company.

With Röhrl out of the equation, the next candidate on Todt's shortlist was Markku Alén, the dazzlingly talented Finn who had anchored Fiat and Lancia's squads for the past five years. Markku enjoyed the Italian lifestyle, however, and demanded a colossal fee to move to France – a figure which Todt had no problem in turning down.

Next on the list was a relative youngster,

BELOW Ari Vatanen (right), chats with championship rival Guy Fréquelin during their showdown at the 1981 RAC Rally. Although his style was far removed from Todt's ideal of a measured, even-headed driver, he would come to lead the Peugeot 205 Turbo 16 squad in 1984. *(McKlein)*

Henri Toivonen, who had matured from a spectacularly fast but rather erratic rookie to become a genuine contender for victory in cars that really had no right to be so far up the order. Toivonen, though, already had an offer from Lancia on the table, and he elected to take it.

Traditionally, French drivers were experts on paved surfaces but lacked the same versatility of the Scandinavians on loose gravel or snow. Guy Fréquelin had been a reliable number one for Talbot but had just agreed to join Opel, and just one other French driver had shown potentially title-winning versatility and that was Michèle Mouton. Having the universally adored Frenchwoman on board would no doubt be popular but, in Todt's view, it would certainly distract from the car and the team in terms of public and media interest.

All of this left one contender to lead the team: 1981 world champion, Ari Vatanen. The mercurial 30-year-old was hardly equipped with the same sort of temperament as Todt; he was a man in love with the thrill of holding a car on the edge and with the response that it drew from the crowds at the roadside. Vatanen was a huge risk for any team to gamble upon, a man who would either win by a mile or destroy the car completely – but there were few options left open.

Todt travelled to Kenya in order to watch the 1983 Safari Rally, where Audi would be running its Quattros for the first time and he was interested to see how the cars might fare. Ari Vatanen was there with the by-now archaic Opel Ascona, and the two men chatted throughout the event. The Safari is an event that requires a measured approach rather than all-out speed, and on this occasion the Finn seized upon the frailty of the Quattros to claim an impressive win – one which convinced Todt that he could be entrusted with leading Peugeot Talbot Sport.

The Peugeot 205 Turbo 16 that had been revealed to the world's press in early 1983 was little more than a rolling shell. Through the year the engine and transmission were evolved and developed in an intensive and fiercely guarded testing programme conducted by Jean-Pierre Nicolas and the engineers. Sadly, they had been forced to conduct this

programme without Des O'Dell's enormous experience behind them, as his wife had died and he had decided to return to Coventry to care for his family.

O'Dell had laid out the basic architecture and instructed the team on design priorities that needed to be considered, such as standardising as many parts as possible (including nuts, bolts and washers) to make servicing the car as easy as possible. The rest of the job, however, would be handed over to a largely inexperienced French group under Jean-Claude Vaucard.

Initial testing took place at the famous old grand prix circuit at Montlhéry to the north of Paris, then on a gravel stage set up at Lardy in the Essonne region of France. Initially the tests gave only cause for concern: the turbo engine was brutally unsophisticated, although the car's weight distribution and cornering habits seemed okay on asphalt. On gravel, however, almost every part of the brakes and suspension broke at one point or another, leading to some hasty redesigning and strengthening work to be carried out.

The core team did their best but it was clear that a car this complex was going to need specialist chassis and turbo engineers to be drafted in. The brief and scope that had been handed to Todt by Jean Boillot and the Peugeot board had always been to maximise the involvement and ownership of Peugeot's

ABOVE In October 1983 the Peugeot 205 Turbo 16 was given its competitive debut on the short, rough stage at Sarlat. Jean-Pierre Nicolas only just made it to the finish, but valuable lessons were learnt. *(Peugeot)*

in-house engineers and to avoid recruiting outside the company wherever possible – but there was also an ever-increasing mountain of money being invested in the programme that Todt needed to justify with success.

In October 1983, the core team had a target of giving the new car its unofficial debut at the annual memorial rally in honour of former Peugeot driver Jean-François Piot, who had been killed in 1980 when the Land Rover he was driving on the Tour of Morocco plunged into a ravine. Jean-Pierre Nicolas and the 205 Turbo 16 made it to the finish of this short gravel rally in Sarlat, but at a considerably reduced pace next to their more traditional competitors. Something needed to be done fast.

The arrival of Jean-Pierre Boudy, formerly head of the Renault F1 turbo programme, was a deliverance in many ways. He got to work immediately on making the engine behave better, increasing the workable rev band and encouraging the turbo to provide a more immediate and less theatrical response. Jean-Claude Vaucard and the rest of the team had been preoccupied with the suspension

components and the strength of the car, making it tough enough but supple, and maintaining both its power-to-weight balance and the cornering prowess that it had shown from the outset.

In late 1983, the team went to Selva in Tuscany where they were able to rent the use of one of the stages used in the Sanremo Rally earlier in the autumn. This test would provide Ari Vatanen and his co-driver Terry Harryman with their first taste of the 205 Turbo 16, and at the end of their first run the Finn turned to look at his co-driver with a sigh. There was no doubt that the car was fast.

Just how fast it was remained to be seen. Vatanen had to leave in order to contest the RAC Rally so Jean-Pierre Nicolas took over. The stage had been driven in dry daylight conditions on the Sanremo event, with Stig Blomqvist setting the fastest time in his Audi Quattro of 2m 06, well clear of his Audi teammates and considerably faster than the best of the Lancias in fourth place.

At night, in the rain, Jean-Pierre Nicolas set off for a timed run to benchmark how much progress had been made and set a time of 2m 06 to equal that of Blomqvist in considerably worse conditions. The team members embraced one another – finally it felt as though they were on the right track.

In January 1984, another ex-Renault F1 man was added to the team's strength, in the form of André de Cortanze. It was by now too late for him to influence the car that would make Peugeot's debut in the World Rally Championship that year and with, as he himself admitted, roughly '0.5% knowledge' of rallying in general it was not the time to start making waves. Where his experience was put to work in 1984 was ensuring that the production quality both in-house and from the many suppliers to the programme was in order, while he would take over the design reins from Jean-Claude Vaucard for the second evolution of the car.

Testing continued throughout the early spring, with Jean Todt pushing hard to ensure that every eventuality might be covered in time for the car's debut on France's round of the 1984 world championship calendar, the 28th annual Tour de Corse.

LEFT The 1983 test hacks were somewhat rudimentary compared with the finished cars of 1984–86 but the lessons that they taught the team were to prove invaluable. *(McKlein)*

BELOW Ari Vatanen put on a performance of measured brilliance to win the 1983 Safari Rally, resisting the urge to press too much too soon and reassuring Jean Todt that he had found his star man. *(McKlein)*

Chapter Two

The competition story

Through two-and-a-half seasons of the World Rally Championship and then on to new challenges thereafter, the Peugeot 205 Turbo 16 set a pace that left onlookers dumbfounded. On every surface, in every weather, it was fast and reliable enough to start as favourite from its first event to its last. In the pomp of Group B rallying there was nothing else like it.

OPPOSITE The long and winding road of rallying is what the Peugeot 205 Turbo 16 was born to conquer – although few could have predicted such dominance. *(McKlein)*

The 1984 World Rally Championship

When the World Rally Championship teams gathered in Monte Carlo at the start of the 1984 season, it appeared as though nothing was going to shake Audi's cast iron grip upon the sport. The Audi Quattro remained as the first and only car to benefit from turbo power and four-wheel-drive traction, and its mastery of loose surfaces, which formed the bulk of the calendar, had seldom been challenged.

Over the two previous seasons, the greatest threat to Audi's dominance had been the ferocity with which Germany's greatest driver, Walter Röhrl, had attacked at every opportunity. Ever since Audi very publicly spurned him as a driver for the team's debut season in 1981, Röhrl had gleefully barred the way to the 1982 drivers' championship and the 1983 manufacturers' championship through sheer force of will and sublime driving talent. Finally, common sense had prevailed in Ingolstadt and Röhrl was brought on board, completing what looked like an insuperable force in rallying. It would look that way right up until the Peugeot 205 Turbo 16 appeared.

The rallying world is small and close-knit, so already there was some trepidation about the storm that was coming from Peugeot Talbot

Sport. For Audi, the Tour de Corse had become its Achilles' heel because the Quattro was a long, heavy car that lacked the sort of nimble handling that its roads required. To this end, the team had arrived in Corsica with what it hoped was a solution to this Corsican conundrum: the Audi Sport Quattro: shorter in the wheelbase and more powerful than ever.

The Peugeots arrived in quite a low-key fashion, despite the rabid interest of the French fans and media. At the start of the event Lancia's expert on Corsica, Italian asphalt specialist Attilio Bettega, took off into a comfortable lead, but soon Ari Vatanen and Peugeot began to close up.

A pitched battle ensued between no fewer than three of the sleek Lancia 037 coupés, with Vatanen dancing through this pack to assume the lead. In contrast, the short-wheelbase Audi was unable to climb higher than sixth place, with Walter Röhrl fending off Peugeot's returning veteran Jean-Pierre Nicolas until the Sport Quattro's engine expired.

Lancia team principal Cesare Fiorio wore a look of resignation: Corsica had been Lancia's fiefdom in recent seasons, but now his team's supercharged coupé was being shown the way home by a little French hatchback. 'It is surely of the latest generation of rally cars', he said. 'That is to say four-wheel-drive central engine, which is a bit of a new technique which

BELOW Peugeot Talbot Sport wheeled out the 205 Turbo 16 to a near-hysterical response from French fans and media, the immaculate white cars looking at home from the outset.
(McKlein)

is being developed by many manufacturers after Audi and the Quattro....'

Vatanen and Harryman continued to stretch their lead until, on the penultimate day, they hit a rock and lost valuable time until the suspension could be repaired. They were able to make up most of the lost time and after hysterical news coverage overnight it seemed that the whole of France was watching, waiting and willing the little car across the line.

And that was the moment when rain began to fall quite heavily and he aquaplaned off the road, barrel-rolling 80 feet into a tree-lined ravine. A dazed Vatanen and co-driver Terry Harryman struggled back up the hillside while their Peugeot burnt to the ground below them.

'I am disappointed', Jean Todt shrugged. 'I am disappointed for the team, for the efforts that were made and everyone started to dream... and then it was crashed against a rock. But it's motor sport....'

It was left to Jean-Pierre Nicolas to ease off and bring the surviving 205 Turbo 16 home in a fine fourth place behind Ragnotti and the Lancias of Miki Biasion and the victorious Markku Alén.

The next event would be the Acropolis Rally – one of the most punishing tests of a car's structural integrity and of its engine and transmission's capacity to absorb the effects of dust, boulders and blistering heat. Much like on an African rally, drivers and co-drivers played the long game in Greece: it was a slog at perhaps 80% of their potential speed, picking their way through to be in contention at the finish.

The Acropolis was Audi territory in which the big, robust Quattros would always be the pre-event favourites, and they lived up to their billing. The little Peugeot was demonstrably easier to drive, skittering over the rugged terrain and allowing both Vatanen and Nicolas the luxury of picking their line through the corners rather than being wrestled through them physically like the big Audis. Eventually, though, both Peugeots were shaken to pieces and Blomqvist duly led Mikkola home to an emphatic result for Audi.

Jean Todt did not trouble himself with the vast expense of travelling to New Zealand or Argentina to gain more experience. Instead, Peugeot Talbot Sport went on a campaign

ABOVE Monsoon conditions on the last morning saw Vatanen aquaplane out of the lead, leaving Jean-Pierre Nicolas to finish a creditable fourth on the new car's debut event. *(McKlein)*

of relentless testing in Europe throughout the summer months to make sure that the weaknesses shown up in those first two events could be eradicated.

Peugeot Talbot Sport would reappear for the 1000 Lakes in Ari Vatanen's home country of Finland. The 1000 Lakes was never an event that Jean-Pierre Nicolas relished, and the decision was taken for just a single entry to be made and for Vatanen to receive the full weight of the team to help him on his way.

Peugeot had spent weeks leading up to

BELOW After two retirements in close succession, neither Ari Vatanen nor Peugeot Talbot Sport was taking any chances in Finland, testing the car for weeks prior to the start – with spectacular results. *(McKlein)*

RIGHT Third time's the charm: Ari Vatanen and Terry Harryman destroyed the competition in Finland, deservedly soaking up the acclaim as the Peugeot 205 Turbo 16 notched up its maiden victory. *(McKlein)*

the event, camped out in the Finnish forests, honing the car to perfection. This included a significant upgrade to the engine, which gained fully 30bhp from the specification used in Corsica and Greece. It also included the complete re-engineering of the suspension, which kept breaking under the relentless jumps and yumps, causing the team to almost despair until the heavier-gauge components became available.

Through this level of preparation, added to Vatanen's natural speed and determination, the 1984 1000 Lakes proved to be a complete rout for Peugeot. Early on Markku Alón took the lead for his beloved Lancia team but then, grabbing the little 205 Turbo 16 by the scruff of its neck, Vatanen won 31 out of 50 special stages.

Alén's frustration was tangible throughout the event, one that he had good cause to feel was his own province. Vatanen couldn't help but tease his fellow countryman in his pursuit of the Peugeot, declaring that: 'Well, in my case, I think I'm just building up slowly. You know, Markku is an Italian so he heats up very quickly!'

There were some who were concerned by the Peugeot's handling when it came to the big jumps in Finland. With the weight of the engine

offset in the rear of the car, it would often throw its tail up in a lopsided manner that demanded every ounce of Vatanen's prodigious talents to catch when it landed – in stark contrast to the Lancias, which flew as gracefully as a Spitfire.

Even the Audis, with their nose-high attitude, seemed to be less hard work over the yumps, and the Quattros did enough to seal the manufacturers' title for 1984 with Blomqvist, steadfastly refusing to relinquish the long-wheelbase car, finishing fourth behind the Lancias of Alén and Toivonen. Once again, the short-wheelbase Audis had faltered but for Peugeot, the 205's wild handling over the jumps would be a problem for another day: a miss is as good as a mile, especially when it ends in victory.

Ari Vatanen, with Terry Harryman alongside him, proudly climbed atop his world-beating new car and they waved their laurels and flowers for the cameras. Jean Todt smiled beatifically and embraced the men who had engineered his vision into reality – now it was time to capitalise upon the advantage that they had painstakingly built to put Peugeot at the pinnacle of rallying around the world.

Perhaps not even Todt could have dared to dream what that 1000 Lakes victory would

usher in for Peugeot, however. Next on the calendar was the Rallye Sanremo – Italy's round of the world championship and an event previewed by the all-important Italian press as a must-win event. The deck was loaded as heavily as possible in the home team's favour, with no fewer than six Lancia 037s in the entry, against which Audi sent only a token entry of two Audi Sport Quattros for Blomqvist and Walter Röhrl.

The Lancias got underway with stage wins for Miki Biasion, Attilio Bettega and Markku Alén on asphalt but then the rally moved on to gravel and Vatanen began to pick up the pace for Peugeot. It would take him until the ninth stage to overhaul the leaders but after that he never looked back, despite a near miss when aquaplaning into a spin in the middle of the night. He would claim a total of 31 stage wins from the 54 completed (two stages being cancelled along the way due to bad weather), ending the rally more than five minutes clear of Bettega's second-placed Lancia.

Peugeot opted out of the gruelling Ivory Coast Rally, in which Stig Blomqvist managed to coax the Audi Sport Quattro through to take its only victory in top-class competition, and thereby claim the drivers' world championship crown. Next would come Britain and the

rigours of the RAC Rally, with a single entry from Peugeot for Ari Vatanen.

With both the drivers' and manufacturers' titles secure, Audi Sport decided against the expense of sending their works team on the event. Vatanen's main competition would come from Audi UK, which had funded an appearance from Hannu Mikkola in its own long-wheelbase Quattro, while also paying Ingolstadt for the loan of a short-wheelbase Sport Quattro that would be driven by Michèle Mouton.

Two privately entered long-wheelbase Quattros were also present, handled by North American champion John Buffum and the rapid young Englishman Malcolm Wilson. The rest of the top entries were made up of rear-drive Opels, Toyotas and Nissans that were unlikely to prove much of a challenge.

For the first 39 stages, Vatanen delivered a command performance on stages that he knew like the back of his hand from his many years of competing in the UK. Then in the middle of the night, disaster struck when he lost concentration and the Peugeot was pitched into a lurid roll. Minus its windscreen, but otherwise undamaged, Vatanen and Harryman got the car going again, but Hannu Mikkola had meanwhile got through to lead.

ABOVE The landslide that started in Finland gained momentum in Italy, with Vatanen humiliating Lancia in front of the partisan press as he strolled to an easy win over the armada of 037s. *(McKlein)*

ABOVE On stages that he knew well, Vatanen could only be beaten by Mikkola on the RAC Rally... and he nearly was. Recovering from an error late in the rally, victory was sealed by a margin of just 41 seconds. *(McKlein)*

BELOW Two French icons – the Peugeot 205 Turbo 16 of Ari Vatanen and Terry Harryman prepares to set off for Monte Carlo from beneath the Tour d'Eiffel. *(McKlein)*

Mikkola was the master of the British forests, a four-time RAC Rally winner and no less adored by the knowledgeable British crowds than Vatanen. It was clear that on this occasion, the once-mighty Quattro was now the underdog, which drew even more support from the home crowd but even their support could do little to hold off the flying Peugeot. Vatanen got back into the lead but then on the final morning the 205 Turbo 16 popped a driveshaft and Mikkola stormed past once again.

When the Peugeot was repaired it would require an all-out attack from Vatanen to close the gap, and what the event lacked in numbers the two great Finnish stars made up for with flair and competitive spirit. At the end, Vatanen crossed the line just 41 seconds ahead of his countryman after more than nine hours of driving at the absolute limit.

Two wins from four rallies was the sort of start that any team would be proud of – any, that is, except one that was run by Jean Todt. He was desperately concerned about Vatanen's ability to lead the team after throwing away his moment of glory in Corsica, breaking the car in Greece and risking what should have been a straightforward win in Britain.

To strengthen his hand, Todt reluctantly stood Jean-Pierre Nicolas down from a driving role, and brought him into the administration of the team, working on testing and the management of the new national championship programmes that would start in Italy, Germany, France and Britain during 1985. In his place arrived two new drivers for the world championship squad: Frenchman Bruno Saby, an asphalt specialist, and another Finn in the bespectacled form of Timo Salonen. It was to prove an inspired choice.

The 1985 World Rally Championship

With three wins from its first five events, Peugeot Talbot Sport arrived in Monte Carlo as the clear favourite for victory on what was always considered a home event by both French teams (not to mention the majority of the rally officials). Not that Jean Todt was taking anything for granted.

Audi had, after all, spent long days and

nights in the Alpes Maritimes trying to master its wildly powerful Sport Quattro, while it was clear that Ford, Lancia, Austin Rover and even Citroën were well advanced with building their own mid-engined four-wheel-drive Group B cars. Todt knew that Audi had squandered much of the colossal advantage it had enjoyed in the first years of the Quattro – and he was utterly determined not to allow Peugeot Talbot Sport any such misadventures.

To this end, he arrived with his full squad of three cars, all of them primed and ready. Against Vatanen, Salonen and Saby stood two Audi Sport Quattros for Walter Röhrl and Stig Blomqvist – these five entries were the only four-wheel-drive Group B cars in the field and there would be little that any of the 112 other entries would offer in terms of resistance.

Heavy snow and ice sat on most of the stages and, as expected, the battle for victory lay between Monte-meister Röhrl and the Peugeot of Vatanen. The German shot off into an early lead with Vatanen keeping a watching brief. Behind them Blomqvist was battling the Lancia 037 of Finnish youngster Henri Toivonen, while Salonen was desperately uncomfortable in the Peugeot and could not find a way to get close to Vatanen's pace.

Bruno Saby's enthusiasm got the better of him and sent him off the road, dropping six minutes in the process, which he was taking his time to make up again.

Vatanen duly assumed command once the rally dropped down into the valleys and on to dry asphalt, building up a four-minute advantage until the checkpoint at Gap. This

was where a combination of errors led to Terry Harryman checking them in early and earning them a draconian eight-minute penalty. This put Röhrl at a four-minute advantage instead, but allowed Vatanen the opportunity to embark on what many still believe to be the greatest drive in the history of rallying.

It took him eight mesmerising stages to catch and pass Röhrl, the denouement coming on live TV when the German elected to start the Col de St Raphael stage on intermediate tyres, knowing that only a third of the stage was covered in snow while the rest was bone dry. Vatanen was on snow tyres and rapidly dispensed with the Quattro's minute-long head start to pass it, then held his advantage while skittering over the asphalt on completely the wrong tyres for the job.

'There is not such a thing as an absolute limit which is a solid one', he said. 'I mean

ABOVE With Saby out and Salonen struggling to find his feet in the Peugeot, Vatanen alone took the fight to Audi's four-time Monte Carlo winner, Walter Röhrl. (McKlein)

BELOW An inspired drive by Ari Vatanen was backed up by impressive support from the entire Peugeot Talbot Sport team to deliver one of the greatest wins in rally history. (McKlein)

it's – the limit is flexible, you can stretch it if it needs to be stretched and it's more... more a psychological thing, really.'

It was to be Peugeot versus Audi once again two weeks later in the snowbound forests of Sweden, with an equally stern test for the French team as it took on Stig Blomqvist in his home event, which he had won a record

ABOVE Ari Vatanen completed a remarkable run of five consecutive victories when he crossed the line at the 1985 Swedish Rally. (McKlein)

BELOW Driving through a tunnel of human bodies was nobody's idea of fun, but crews knew what to expect in Portugal, where rallying was like a religion. Timo Salonen finally got the Peugeot tailored to his comfort and delivered a consummate victory. (McKlein)

seven times previously. Blomqvist would prove to be no less an implacable foe than Röhrl had been in Monte Carlo, and it is a measure of his performance that with no trouble for Vatanen or Peugeot, the Swede finished only 1 minute and 49 seconds in arrears.

Five consecutive wins for Vatanen and Peugeot was an unprecedented achievement. In Sweden, the second event in a row, Timo Salonen had also finished in third place and he was beginning to find some real confidence in the 205 Turbo 16. To complete the puzzle, he requested that the team make some modifications to the steering rack on his new car when it was being prepared for the next event in Portugal – which would prove decisive.

Portugal was an event that both Walter Röhrl and Stig Blomqvist enjoyed, while its combination of gravel stages with smooth asphalt gave some crumb of hope to the two-wheel-drive Lancias. Vatanen made his by-now traditional measured start and let Röhrl take the fight to the Lancias but on the gravel his suspension gave out and that was that.

But then there was Timo Salonen, who had won two of the first five stages as he settled in to the car and proceeded to shadow Röhrl's every move. When the road surface was loose the Audis held sway and when there was asphalt beneath them the Lancias galloped off but Salonen simply stayed close to whoever was fastest and assiduously put himself in contention before launching a devastating run of six stage wins at the end of the event, thereby taking victory.

It was a thoroughly professional takedown of all the biggest names in the sport by the quietest man in the service park. It was also the sort of performance that Jean Todt truly relished, for while swashbuckling Ari Vatanen was the fans' favourite, his inability to conceive of a margin for error caused his boss considerable unease. Salonen would never inspire the same sort of passion as Vatanen, but he was exactly the sort of man that Todt had been seeking.

Kenya beckoned and with it the most gruelling adventure on the World Rally Championship calendar. Peugeot Talbot Sport had never before subjected its cars to the demands of Africa, but Peugeot itself it had taken six previous victories in the space of 15 years with its rugged 404 and 504 saloons and was keen to reclaim its crown. Three 205 Turbo 16s were suitably beefed-up with heavier, stronger bodies and detuned but more durable engines.

Vatanen showed he was able to run at the pace of the front runners but his suspension fell apart and finally the engine lost all of its water, so he was out of the running. Bruno Saby's car also proved to be rather less equal to the job, breaking the chassis on a particularly brutal stage.

It was left to Timo Salonen, with his long experience in Africa as a member of Toyota's team, to trudge onward at a much reduced pace compared with his teammates. On almost every stage, the 205 Turbo 16 threatened to fall apart but with the quietly insistent coaxing and cajoling of its driver it reached the finish in seventh place, thereby upholding Peugeot's honour.

One year on from the team's debut, Peugeot Talbot Sport returned to Corsica with two standard cars for Vatanen and Salonen while Bruno Saby was entrusted with giving the new 'Evolution 2' car its first competitive start. Featuring significant weight reduction, increased power and aerodynamic wings on the front and rear, the new car looked incredible.

Peugeot's biggest challenger was expected to be Walter Röhrl, who had once again been hard at work on honing the unruly Audi Sport Quattro, which now featured even more power and a water cooling system for its brakes. But Lancia could never be discounted in Corsica, and it arrived with lightened 037s for Markku Alén, Attilio Bettega and Miki Biasion.

Nevertheless, it was not Peugeot, Audi or Lancia that set the early pace but instead the irrepressible Jean Ragnotti at the wheel of the latest evolution of the Renault 5 Turbo, the so-called Maxiturbo. Ragnotti won the first stage and assumed a lead that he would never lose. Vatanen closed up on him but then the rally came to a tragic halt when Bettega went off on the fourth stage.

The Italian's Lancia ran wide on a right-hander and dived into the trees. Although the frail little coupé was practically cleaved in two by the accident, Bettega's fate was in fact sealed when one of the branches lanced into the cockpit and killed him outright – his

traumatised co-driver Maurizio Perissinot being physically unscathed in the incident. Immediately the two sister cars were withdrawn but the rally carried on.

In his pursuit of the flying Ragnotti, Vatanen won ten stages but then disaster struck just when he was about to overhaul the leader. The Finn misjudged a sharp left-hander and the

ABOVE Making its debut on the Safari Rally showed that the Peugeot 205 Turbo 16 was not insuperable. Both Vatanen and Saby's cars fell to bits, while Salonen crossed the line in the remains of his. *(McKlein)*

BELOW Attilio Bettega set out to take the fight to the Peugeots in Corsica but was to lose his life in a fierce battle for the lead. *(McKlein)*

RIGHT For the second year running, Vatanen crashed out in Corsica. All the more galling to the team was that victory fell to the Renault 5 Turbo of Jean Ragnotti, to the delight of the home crowd. *(McKlein)*

little Peugeot flipped up and over into a high-speed barrel roll that carried it off the hillside and into the trees far below.

Dazed but alive, Vatanen and Harryman clambered out of the ravine while Ragnotti and the Renault surged onward. Salonen suffered an almost unheard-of engine failure and Röhrl's Audi fried its brakes, leaving Bruno Saby and the new 205 Turbo 16 E2 to follow his countryman to a somewhat muted podium with Bernard Béguin's Porsche 911 coming home in third place.

Only two of the older-specification cars were sent to Greece for the Acropolis Rally. Two Audi Sport Quattros were dispatched for Röhrl and Blomqvist and these were joined by a pair of Lancias for Andrea Zanussi and Mauro Pregliasco as token resistance, but there was never a great deal of doubt about the outcome. Peugeot led from start to finish, although Vatanen went out on the very first stage with broken steering and it fell to Salonen to calmly and unhurriedly claim the honours.

Peugeot Talbot Sport made its first venture to New Zealand four weeks later for a rally that was as close as any in nature to the fabled 1000 Lakes. With two Finns at the top of their game, the prospect of a mouth-watering battle

LEFT Timo Salonen coaxed his Peugeot through the rubble-strewn stages of the Acropolis to victory and followed up with another win here in New Zealand, one of his strongest events over many years. *(McKlein)*

between Vatanen as the established star and Salonen as the unflappable points leader did not disappoint. Salonen won 17 stages to Vatanen's 16, with the Audis of Röhrl and Blomqvist mustering 17 more between them.

Peugeot's notional number two claimed his third victory of the season compared with Vatanen's two wins, and his measured approach had brought an additional 28 points where the star man had scored none. The challenge was not insurmountable if Vatanen wanted the honour of being Peugeot's first world champion but he was going to have to work hard in the events still to come.

Three of the original-spec 205 Turbo 16s made their way to Argentina for the next round, where Salonen and Vatanen would be joined by none other than former Formula 1 star turned political figure Carlos Reutemann. Most of the competition was fairly notional, with the very obvious exception of Stig Blomqvist.

Audi's technical chief Roland Gumpert and his team had wildly re-engineered their disappointing Audi Sport Quattro to create the S1 by throwing all of the car's ancillaries into the boot to try and help its weight distribution while adding yet more power. To try and translate all this work into traction, a gigantic snow plough of a front wing had been fitted and paired with a high-mounted rear wing.

The new Quattro was undoubtedly wild but it was still fundamentally a production car that had been bullied into the most infeasible shape by its creators, while the Peugeot 205 Turbo 16 was a thoroughbred competition car

that happened to bear a strong resemblance to the humble hatchback. The revised Audi was prodigiously fast but the Peugeots took off into the distance at the start, with Vatanen winning the first stage.

On the second stage, Vatanen was pressing on and absolutely flat in top when he came over a yump and the Peugeot became airborne in its typical style, throwing its backside up in the air with the weight transfer of the engine tilting it to the driver's side. Travelling at around 120mph, the nose came down into a dip in the road on Vatanen's side of the car and hurled it into a sickening series of end-over-end cartwheels.

So violent was the first impact that Vatanen's seat broke free of its mountings, and as the car tumbled into the scrubland its helpless occupant suffered severe leg and back injuries. The team's chase helicopter touched down as a crowd of spectators sought to free him and tend to his injured co-driver Harryman.

For Ari Vatanen, a long and traumatic journey lay ahead, fighting first for life and then for a return to the sport that he loved. Timo Salonen, meanwhile, drove on to claim an untroubled victory after Stig Blomqvist's mighty new 20-valve engine blew up, leaving Austrian national championship regular Wilfried Wiedener to take the runner-up spot in his old long-wheelbase Quattro, almost 15 minutes adrift. Carlos Reutemann took third place, an impressive achievement for an F1 driver, even if he was more than half an hour behind the winner at the finish.

ABOVE Trailing Salonen by 28 points in the drivers' standings, Vatanen had to take victory in Argentina to stay in contention, but was caught out over a jump and both he and Terry Harryman were seriously injured. *(McKlein)*

ABOVE Former
Brabham, Ferrari, Lotus
and Williams F1 star
Carlos Reutemann
joined Peugeot for
his home event in
Argentina, coming
home third. *(Peugeot)*

drivers' and manufacturers' titles rather than drag out the uncertainty. Timo Salonen was now de facto team leader and alongside him Jean Todt drafted in Kalle Grundel, a young Swede who had been the star of production-based Group A rallying in recent seasons before utterly dominating the German national championship in a Peugeot Germany-funded 205 Turbo 16.

On the opening stage, Grundel thundered through the rain down a long straight but was unsettled by a yump in the road and ended up thumping into a few spectators – fortunately without injury. His 205's steering was broken, however, and he would lose a barrel load of time until it was repaired.

Salonen had set the fastest time on the first stage but then Markku Alén rolled the dice in his Lancia 037, driving out of his skin in the rear-drive car to claim two stage wins and the overall lead. Another man on a mission was Stig Blomqvist, the only contender with even a ghost of a chance to beat Salonen in the drivers' championship points, who took the mighty be-winged Quattro and hurled it through the forests.

Remarkably, the top three drivers in their very different cars all managed to tie for the win of Stage 11 but from then on Salonen began to edge away from the pack. At the finish he could look back on 20 stage wins from the 49 that were run, with his margin of victory just 48 seconds – but he sealed both

It was no coincidence that when the teams regrouped in Finland for the 1000 Lakes, Peugeot Talbot Sport brought with it a full complement of the latest 205 Turbo 16 E2s. It was true that the extra power and lighter weight would be beneficial on the fastest event of the year, but many in the service park felt that the huge rear wing on the new model brought a significant improvement in the car's trajectory in flight – something which may have spared Vatanen and Harryman such an horrific ordeal. If there was one thing that could be relied upon in Finland, it was plenty of time in the air.

The weather was grim and there was a businesslike air in the Peugeot camp, where the mood was one of determination to seal the

RIGHT Timo Salonen
continued his run of
victories by claiming a
fourth consecutive win
at home in Finland, his
fifth of the year, which
sealed the all-important
manufacturers' title as
well as his own drivers'
championship crown.
(McKlein)

the drivers' and manufacturers' crowns.

For Jean Todt and the team it was 'Mission: accomplished' and his audacious prediction from 1981 was, so far, completely on track. Winning the world championship with three rounds remaining allowed him to turn his attentions towards the 1986 season, and there was plenty to be concerned about. For one thing, he would have to replace Ari Vatanen, and neither Kalle Grundel or Bruno Saby could realistically be expected to fill those shoes. Adding to his concerns were the fact that Audi was spending a fantastic sum of money on getting the Quattros back on the pace, while Lancia, Ford and Austin Rover all had their mid-engine four-wheel-drive cars on the cusp of joining the fray. Adding another, albeit lesser, potential spanner in the works was the fact that sister company Citroën had gone ahead with its own rival to the 205 Turbo 16, which could provide an unwelcome internal distraction within the PSA family, whether it won or lost.

The next round was in Italy and the combined asphalt/gravel epic of Sanremo. Peugeot sent two E2 cars for Salonen and Saby while a third car, an original Turbo 16 operated by Peugeot Italia, was entered for its national championship driver, Giovanni del Zoppo, and co-driver, Elisabetta Tognana. Lancia had five 037s at the start of its home event but all eyes were on the Audi Sport Quattro S1 of Walter Röhrl, who had made this event the sole focus of a gigantic testing programme.

With the 20-valve engine turning out far in excess of 500bhp and a raft of detail tweaks made to the design and construction of the car, Röhrl's Audi was howling like Brünnhilde atop Siegfried's funeral pyre. The mercurial Röhrl was at his peerless best, with the result that he won 29 of the 43 stages run to claim victory by more than six minutes, his nearest contenders being Salonen and Lancia's Henri Toivonen with a mere seven stage wins apiece.

After taking such a beating from Röhrl's Wagnerian performance in Italy, Peugeot did not trouble itself with voyaging to the Ivory Coast, which was left to the Japanese manufacturers to argue over. The final round would come in Britain for the RAC Rally with

ABOVE **Sheer force of will powered Walter Röhrl to what would be Audi's final world championship win on the 1985 Sanremo, beating back Salonen's Peugeot and a tide of Lancias to take a truly astounding victory.** (McKlein)

what felt like rather a depleted effort: Salonen joined by Grundel and Peugeot UK's national championship entry of Mikael Sundström and Paul White in their early-spec Turbo 16.

All eyes were on two newcomers to the series: the Lancia Delta S4s and the MG Metro 6R4s, both of which were mid-engined four-wheel-drive thoroughbreds wearing hatchback bodyshells, like the Peugeot.

Lancia had elected to build an engine that was both supercharged and turbocharged in an

BELOW **Lancia joined the four-wheel-drive club on the 1985 RAC Rally with its awe-inspiring Delta S4. The supercharged and turbocharged cars were the class of the field throughout.** (McKlein)

effort to boost power while minimising throttle lag. Austin Rover deployed a throaty V6 engine with no forced induction at all, hoping that the consequent shortfall in power would be made up for by increased responsiveness and torque. Both designs looked astonishing and proved to be shatteringly fast out of the box.

Elsewhere in the field, unnoticed by all but those with a keen ear, Walter Röhrl was present with a new variation of the Audi Sport Quattro S1. This car was fitted with a version of the Porsche PDK transmission that allowed completely seamless gear changes to be made semi-automatically. Gone was the staccato sound of the car being pushed up through its gears in favour of a steady, powerful roar that accompanied unsettlingly fast acceleration.

It was an electrifying competition in which the Peugeots were merely bit-part players.

Both Mikael Sundström and Kalle Grundel crashed out, while Salonen's engine played up and eventually succumbed to a terminal loss of oil pressure. It hardly mattered, as none of the French cars was in contention at any stage. It seemed that everyone could only look on as the Lancias took off into the distance, with Henri Toivonen eventually holding off Markku Alén for the win.

Home-grown hero Tony Pond raised the rafters with a career-defining drive to third place in the Metro 6R4. It was also notable that Pond by himself claimed as many stage wins as the three Peugeots combined – although Jean Todt was quick to suggest that this was merely a demonstration of how much Britain's ban on weeks-long reconnaissance favoured the local drivers. The taste of victory seemed like a distant memory as the team returned to Paris and began its preparations for the 1986 season.

The 1986 World Rally Championship

In the space of 13 rallies, Peugeot Talbot Sport had gone from a virgin team with an unproven car to holding both the drivers' and manufacturers' titles of the World Rally Championship. It had put the Audi Quattro to the sword and stolen a march on all its Group B competitors but now that they were getting up to speed it looked like a hard-fought season lay ahead as the field set off for the Monte Carlo Rally.

Jean Todt took a leaf out of Lancia's book and did his best to stack the deck against the opposing teams. Defending champion Timo Salonen was there, as was Bruno Saby. Joining them were two new faces in the Peugeot camp: young Finnish talent Juha Kankkunen, a winner with Toyota on both African rallies the previous season, and the 1982 world championship runner-up, Michèle Mouton.

Austin Rover was in place with its MG Metro 6R4s, and so too was Citroën with its own four-whee- drive turbocharged cars, the BX 4TCs. To say that the arrival of a challenger from within the PSA family was unwelcome would be an understatement, but Citroën remained fiercely independent. In the end, the bulky

BXs offered no threat to Todt's team beyond its impact on the PSA balance sheet. Audi was also back with its Sport Quattro S1s for Walter Röhrl and Hannu Mikkola, the last men standing in a greatly reduced effort for 1986.

For the second event in succession, however, there was no answer to the Lancia Delta S4 or Henri Toivonen. Lancia's trio of Toivonen, Miki Biasion and Markku Alén enjoyed a race of their own in the early stages. Part of their advantage lay in their unique supply of Pirelli tyres, perfectly attuned to the S4, while Michelin had to service the Audis, MGs and Peugeots on the ever-changing surfaces.

Lancia and Pirelli even had such an advantage that they could send a tyre van out to the middle of longer stages, which were both snowbound and dry, for an impromptu tyre swap to the appropriate rubber.

Eventually, Lancia's reliability began to go awry. Alén's engine then imploded and Biasion fell away with a misfire. Meanwhile, Walter Röhrl summoned up another Wagnerian charge from his brutal Audi Sport Quattro and began tearing lumps out of Toivonen's lead until his team made a series of catastrophic tyre choices and he slithered down the order.

At Peugeot, Saby had gone off the road, new boy Kankkunen had been waylaid by electrical problems and Mouton's engine had failed. This left Salonen charging after Toivonen, with Todt

doing his part by applying pressure on Michelin to focus its efforts on the only car that could now stop Toivonen and his Pirellis.

As the majority of stages were being run twice, both Saby and Kankkunen were used as guinea pigs on different tyre combinations in order to ensure that Salonen had the optimum setup for the second pass on each stage. His pursuit was aided when Toivonen's car was hit by a spectator (ironically driving a Peugeot), on one of the road sections, which completely bowed the car's chassis and forced the Finn to adjust his driving style to get to the end.

This problem, and a couple of punctures, briefly handed Salonen the lead, but Toivonen launched an all-out attack to claim a remarkable victory from Salonen and the two Audis of Mikkola and Röhrl.

Next came Sweden, which would be the first time that Juha Kankkunen had ever taken

ABOVE Citroën arrived with a Group B car vastly different in design to its sister brand, Peugeot. It was also vastly different in terms of performance. *(McKlein)*

LEFT Timo Salonen, Peugeot and Michelin were pipped to the post by Henri Toivonen, Lancia and Pirelli in what was a truly spectacular clash of the titans. Audi's Hannu Mikkola, in third, shared in their jubilation. *(McKlein)*

ABOVE Piling pressure on Peugeot was the arrival of Ford with its long-awaited RS200 Group B car, which proved to be competitive from the first stage in Sweden. *(McKlein)*

BELOW Stages were in chaos as fans were permitted to run riot on the opening morning of Rally Portugal. Here Juha Kankkunen pushes the tide of humanity to the back of his mind and presses onwards. *(McKlein)*

part on the event. Making its worldwide debut on the event was Ford's remarkable RS200 Group B car, which like the Peugeots and Lancias featured a mid-mounted four-wheel-drive layout.

The major difference was that the Ford's body was not based on any standard production car but instead had a bespoke coupé shell (albeit with certain aspects of production cars, most notably the humble Sierra's windscreen and pillars). With Stig Blomqvist, the undisputed master of Sweden, at the wheel of the lead car and Peugeot's Swedish refugee Kalle Grundel in the second, this new effort posed an entirely new threat to the established order.

It had taken more than 30 years and the advent of four-wheel-drive for the first non-Swede to win the event, when Hannu Mikkola took honours for Audi in the Quattro's debut season of 1981. Five years later, Juha

Kankkunen became the first foreign driver to win in Sweden on his debut appearance with a drive of supreme confidence that shook the established order to its core.

Kankkunen drove imperiously to victory, his nearest challengers being Toivonen and Salonen but they both went out, leaving Markku Alén to take second at the finish. In third place came Grundel in the Ford RS200, and between them the Ford drivers had claimed six stage wins, which certainly gave pause for thought. But the moment belonged to Juha Kankkunen and deservedly so.

A little less than a month later, the ice and snow of the first two rounds seemed like a distant memory as the field regrouped in Estoril for the Rally Portugal. For years, this event had been one of the wildest on the calendar, with fans lining the roadside and attempting to touch the cars as they passed. With Group B now at its zenith, with Audi, Peugeot, Lancia and now Ford wheeling out potentially victorious cars there was an even greater frenzy, and right from the start the drivers and co-drivers were wide-eyed.

On the first stage, Timo Salonen's Peugeot hit a cameraman as he tried to stay in front of the seething masses and broke the man's leg. Then on the fourth stage, disaster struck.

Among the lead runners was three-time Portuguese national champion Joaquin Santos, at the wheel of a brand-new Ford RS200. As he came over a crest, barely a kilometre from the start, he discovered that his countrymen were spilling out right on his intended line. He braked and tried to steer around them only to discover that the road was covered in sand and dust that many thousands of feet had tracked onto the asphalt and he lost control.

The crowd on the right-hand side of the road was five or six deep, backed up against a deep ditch. Santos had the steering turned hard left but nothing worked and he ploughed straight into the wall of humanity. It was carnage: the Ford's front end being torn to pieces by the weight of the bodies, spinning through the crowd until it came to rest in the ditch.

The next driver through stopped and then, appalled by the scene, drove on to try and get the officials to cancel the stage and send help. Despite his best efforts, the stage was not stopped by the disbelieving officials until 11 further cars had left the start line, causing more delays in getting treatment to the casualties. Some of the rally crews stopped to try and give aid but were chased off by enraged fans. It was a scene of pure bedlam.

Four people died at the scene and more than 30 were injured. Another six are believed to have succumbed to their injuries. Santos and his co-driver were bewildered and beyond grief. Ford withdrew all of its cars with immediate effect. The rest of the manufacturer team drivers from Audi, Peugeot, Lancia and Austin Rover were shepherded together by Walter Röhrl and took up residence in Rally HQ, refusing to go back to their cars until the crowd control was at an acceptable level.

The Portuguese authorities and FISA were enraged by this mutiny and the implication that they were somehow to blame for the tragedy. It would be a tense stand-off (not assisted by Lancia boss Cesare Fiorio demanding that his drivers return to their cars, by force if necessary). In the end, the drivers' mutiny held fast and after six hours the eleven remaining works cars were withdrawn from the Rally Portugal.

The Safari came next at the end of the month, with Peugeot the only team to send four-wheel-drive cars. After the disappointment of their African debut in 1985, Jean Todt had employed five-time Safari winner Shekhar

Mehta to help develop the 205 Turbo 16 for the event. Lancia, meanwhile, felt that its two-wheel-drive 037s, suitably beefed up for the arduous African roads, were better suited to the event than its precious new S4s.

Toyota was the hot favourite with its rugged two-wheel-drive Celicas and its lead crew was former world champion, Björn Waldegård, and co-driver, Fred Gallagher. Gallagher had won the previous year's Safari alongside Juha Kankkunen, who headed the Peugeot entry for 1986, and was joined by Mehta in the second 205 Turbo 16.

In the end the Toyotas finished first, second and fourth, with Markku Alén's Lancia coming home in third. The Peugeots were fast but still too frail to compete for victory, limping home in a distant fifth for Kankkunen with Mehta coming home in eighth after countless delays.

Returning to Europe for the Tour de Corse, a somewhat depleted entry saw only Lancia, Austin Rover and Renault take on the Peugeots at the head of a colossal entry of French cars in the smaller classes. The three works 205 Turbo 16 E2s were entered for Timo Salonen, Bruno Saby and Michèle Mouton, who was guest driving in the midst of a storming season in the German Rally Championship for Peugeot.

Saby made the early running but was then overhauled by teammate Salonen before Henri Toivonen lit the afterburners on his Lancia

BELOW Peugeot beefed up the 205 Turbo 16 for a return to the Safari Rally in 1986. Both Juha Kankkunen and Shehkar Mehta made it to the finish in their cars, but they were plagued by delays. *(McKlein)*

ABOVE Bruno Saby managed to deliver the Tour de Corse, the French round of the World Rally Championship, to Peugeot – but there would be no celebrations. *(McKlein)*

ABOVE RIGHT Juha Kankkunen's season accelerated with back-to-back victories on the Acropolis Rally and here in New Zealand. It was an astounding season for a relatively inexperienced driver, particularly when paired with a driver of Salonen's calibre. *(McKlein)*

and streaked off into the distance. Salonen rolled when he tried to pass Alén's Lancia in the middle of a stage after the Italian car developed a fault. Out in front, Toivonen's lead over Saby stretched to nearly three minutes but then on the 18th stage disaster struck.

Rounding a tightening left-hander, Toivonen's Lancia ran off the road, hitting a low stone wall that flipped the car over as it fell into the tree-lined ravine below, coming to rest upside-down wedged between the cliff face and the trees. Almost instantly the car exploded with a noise that reverberated through the valley, and both Toivonen and his co-driver Sergio Cresto perished in the inferno.

Bruno Saby was the next car through and he stopped where the pillar of black smoke and flame rose up past the roadside to try and give assistance. Seeing that there was no hope, both he and the next car through, the Renault of François Chatriot, raced off to the nearest marshal's post to get word out to get the stage cleared for the emergency services to move in.

The rally would continue for the final day, with the Lancia team withdrawing the remaining Delta S4s of Alén and Biasion and leaving Saby to come home 13 minutes clear of Chatriot. Peugeot had finally won its home event at the third time of asking, but there was to be no joy in the achievement.

By the time that the teams gathered in Athens for the Acropolis Rally, Audi had confirmed its departure from the World Rally Championship on the grounds of safety (omitting to mention

that its cars were no longer competitive). Ford had meanwhile suffered a second fatal accident with the RS200, when F1 driver Marc Surer, competing in the German national championship, had gone off and hit a tree.

Surer was badly injured and his co-driver, Michel Wyder, perished in the resulting inferno. This accident, so soon after Toivonen's death, sealed the fate of Group B and its planned successor, Group S. FIA president Jean-Marie Balestre, under fire for the organisational failures that precipitated the Portuguese disaster, put the blame squarely on the cars. He declared that Group B cars would be illegal from the start of 1987, that Group S would be scrapped and that production-based Group A would become the primary class – causing a political maelstrom to ensue (see Chapter 6).

Three Peugeots were entered for Salonen, Kankkunen and Saby, taking on a trio of Lancias for Alén, Biasion and Swedish newcomer Mikael Ericsson, recruited from the Group A class. Ford brought its two works RS200s for Kalle Grundel and Stig Blomqvist, and although there were no MG Metros, the two Citroën BX 4TCs were present to complete one of the largest Group B entry lists on record.

Grundel led the first three stages for Ford before Salonen's consistency edged him ahead. Both Grundel and Blomqvist continued to threaten but both cars eventually succumbed to the terrain. So too did the Lancias of Alén and Ericsson and both Citroëns, leaving Miki Biasion to make token resistance to the two Peugeots, until Salonen broke his suspension and twisted

LEFT The prodigal son returned when underutilised Ford star Stig Blomqvist took the chance to drive for Peugeot in Argentina and Finland, bringing home valuable manufacturers' points on each occasion. *(McKlein)*

the chassis, handing Kankkunen the win as Saby took a distant third.

Kankkunen won again in New Zealand, where the two lead Peugeots journeyed together with all three of the Lancias. On this event the Lancias had no answer to the pace of the 205 Turbo 16s and a thoroughly entertaining internecine battle ensued between the Peugeot Talbot Sport men that was only resolved when Salonen was hit by a car in regular traffic and had to claw his way back up to fifth at the finish.

This result meant that Salonen's title hopes were all-but over, and he elected to miss the next round in Argentina. In his place came Stig Blomqvist, on loan from a Ford squad that had no plans other than contesting their 'home' event on Britain's RAC Rally. Blomqvist duly shone, taking third place behind the rampant Lancias of Biasion and Alén to protect Peugeot's points advantage after Kankkunen's suspension broke.

In Finland for the 1000 Lakes it was Peugeot's turn to dominate and this time Timo Salonen had the edge over the rest of the team. With the manufacturers' championship as his priority, Jean Todt refused to slow Salonen down even while Juha Kankkunen was closing up in second place, desperate for the five additional points to add towards the drivers' title. Salonen thereby scored his first win of the year, and in so doing delivered the second consecutive manufacturers' title for Peugeot.

Neither Peugeot nor Lancia travelled to the Ivory Coast and so the next event for the

BELOW Timo Salonen's quiet year stepped up a notch at home in Finland, where he took his first win of the year and sealed Peugeot's second successive manufacturers' title. *(McKlein)*

four-wheel-drive cars came at the Italian round in Sanremo. In the end, the event only really served to heap more ignominy upon the World Rally Championship – although there was one ray of sunshine in that Ari Vatanen was present and driving a Peugeot 205 Turbo 16 as the Course Car to open each stage.

Peugeot and Lancia sent four cars apiece – only the lone MG Metro 6R4 of Tony Pond offering a challenge. Any hope of another classic battle between the French and Italians was truncated when Peugeot was deemed to be running with illegal aerodynamic aids.

Since the Tour de Corse, the underbodies

of the 205 Turbo 16s had been fitted with parts that looked like aerodynamic skirts, but were in fact homologated as extra protection for the sump and fuel tank from potential stone damage. A dispute erupted, which only came to an end when the Peugeots were thrown out of the results altogether at the end of the third of four days (with Juha Kankkunen in a very convincing lead).

A maximum score for Lancia and its team leader Markku Alén had the knock-on effect of keeping the drivers' and manufacturers' title race wide open between Lancia and Peugeot / Alén and Kankkunen. The international press went berserk with conspiracy theories while the Italian press spoke of justice being served. In the days that followed, protest and counter-protest, not to mention the odd legal challenge, were zooming overhead like an artillery barrage, while down in the trenches the troops were preparing for mud and thunder on the RAC Rally.

Stig Blomqvist was back in a Ford and he set the early pace on the 'Mickey Mouse' spectator stages before Kankkunen went on the attack. As the last hurrah of Group B at a traditional venue, and with only the long trek out to Washington State in the USA to follow, all of the manufacturers bar Citroën were on the entry list. No fewer than seven MG Metro 6R4s were entered, to the delight of the home crowd, including one car for Henri Toivonen's younger brother Harri that drew considerable crowd support.

It was all about the battle between Peugeot and Lancia, however, and it was an absolute thriller. Kankkunen's lead was overhauled by Alén, then Salonen took over, then Lancia's new boy Mikael Ericsson found himself at the front. Kankkunen and Ericsson traded the lead but then both hit trouble and Salonen was able to notch up his first win of the year, with Alén finishing second, Kankkunen third and Peugeot UK driver Mikael Sundström fourth.

Thanks to the tireless efforts of North American rally champion John Buffum, the Olympus Rally in Washington State was added to the World Rally Championship calendar, offering an event rather like the RAC Rally in terms of its mud and forestry content. Within a few years, Olympia would be world famous as the home of grunge rock but in 1986 it was a rugged logging town with a rugged climate, far removed from most people's idea of America's bright lights.

Peugeot and Lancia sent two cars each – Kankkunen being joined by American driver Jon Woodner in the second car while Alén was teamed with Italian debutante Paolo Alessandrini. Their main competition would come from John Buffum in an Audi Sport Quattro – the earlier short-wheelbase variant without the wild modifications of the S1, which had previously been driven to victory on the Pikes Peak hill climb by Michèle Mouton.

Predictably the rally was Kankkunen vs. Alén and after the Peugeot set the early pace it was the Lancia that then very gently eased its way ahead and onwards to take the win. Buffum's Audi was third, almost 24 minutes adrift, and Alessandrini brought his Lancia home sixth behind the two works Toyotas. Group B rallying ended with a whimper that few people heard in the dark forests of Washington – but it was about to go out with an almighty bang.

The provisional results of the 1986 FIA World Rally Championship for drivers saw Markku Alén provisionally declared the winner with 124 points to Kankkunen's 118. However, Peugeot's protest over being kicked out of the Sanremo still had to be decided.

Peugeot's protest was lodged with the Italian sporting authorities which had administered the Rallye Sanremo, and after due consideration of the fact that their own scrutineers had passed the Peugeots fit to start the rally, and had allowed them to run three-quarters of the event's duration, they would withdraw the exclusion. However, because the Peugeots had then been prevented from completing the rally, the results would stand as they were.

It was left to the FIA to intervene. Rather than ratify the Italians' findings, president Jean-Marie Balestre declared the officials to be 'comedians' and simply declared the result in Sanremo to be void. This took 20 points from Alén's total and handed the drivers' championship to Juha Kankkunen – while at the same time Balestre fined the Italian sporting authorities $20,000 for their ineptitude and banned them from organising anything for six months.

That very same evening, the FIA held its

annual gala awards ceremony in Paris for all of the many champions across the wide variety of disciplines over which it presided. Juha Kankkunen only just made it in time, and was a little bit the worse for wear (see Chapter 6).

New horizons

Peugeot had no Group A cars that could hope to compete with the likes of the Lancia Delta HF Turbo or the Ford Sierra Cosworth and it had precious little budget to support the development of a wildly expensive homologation special. The Peugeot 205 Turbo 16 had done its job on the World Rally Championship stage and sales of the 205 road car were booming around the world as a result – but this did not mean that Jean Todt and his team would be idle.

A number of Peugeot's national importers had been making enquiries about the availability of 205 Turbo 16s for their rallycross programmes. So it was that, with works support, Seppo Niittymäki won Division 2 of the FIA European Rallycross Championship in 1987 at the wheel of a fairly standard Peugeot 205 Turbo 16 E2.

This achievement was then followed by arguably the greatest of all the Peugeot rallycross stars, Matti Alamäki, who won three straight Division 2 titles in 1988–90. At first, Alamäki went all-out for power and managed to see 900bhp on the dyno – for almost exactly one second until there was a very large bang. Urban legend repeatedly claims that this figure was standard but in fact the flying

ABOVE Group B cars were not permitted in the World Rally Championship but they were welcomed in rallycross. From 1987 to 1990, Peugeot 205 Turbo 16s were among the most potent cars in the field and Matti Alamäki, pictured in 1990, won three European championships. *(McKlein)*

Finn seldom ran more than an up-rated version of the final specification engine used by the works team, running 600–650bhp, depending upon the level of boost.

France was also a hugely enthusiastic rallycross nation, and here too the 205 Turbo 16 E2s were put to work. Former Peugeot Talbot driver (and future head of Peugeot's competition department) Guy Fréquelin claimed the 1988 French series title, and was followed by Philippe Wambergue in 1989 and Jean-Manuel Beuzelin in 1990.

But what of the works rally team itself? Well, soon after the announcement that Group B was to cease as the premier rally category, Jean Todt was already on the lookout for new worlds to conquer with his remarkable little cars. Peugeot Talbot Sport had invested

considerable time and money on travelling to Kenya for the Safari Rally in 1985 and again in 1986, when African rally legend Shekhar Mehta had done the development work. The result was a heavier, detuned 205 Turbo 16 with longer suspension travel, and it was this car to which Todt's attentions were first turned.

By October of 1986, while the battle with Lancia for the last Group B world championship was boiling away, a highly modified version of the Safari-spec car was rolled out of the workshop. It was considerably longer and taller than its world championship sisters because the front monocoque and the rear spaceframe sat 30cm apart and into the gap a 350-litre fuel tank had been placed, while the whole vehicle sat on suspension capable of tackling the dunes of the Sahara Desert.

Free from the constraints of formal rallying, the revised car also had a new engine based upon the 1.9-litre Peugeot XU9 engine. In this trim, Todt was laying plans for Peugeot to go to Dakar the quick way with what became known as the 205 Turbo 16 Grand Raid.

The Paris–Dakar Rally Raid had been founded in the late 1970s as an amateur competition among French adventurers who drove through the old French colonies of Algeria and Senegal to conquer the Sahara Desert with a motor race. It was a rudimentary event with rudimentary rules for classes of cars, motorcycles and trucks – until Porsche arrived in 1986 and won with its four-wheel-drive Group B supercar, the 959.

Porsche's 1986 success was the fourth in a series of foreign victories on the event, and French honour needed to be restored. So it was that on New Year's Day 1987, a well-drilled platoon of Peugeot's elite motor sport team set off from Paris to cover the 13,000km epic with the aim of conquering the Sahara.

The entry was led by none other than Ari Vatanen, making his return to competition after the long months of recovery from his near-fatal crash in Argentina. Alongside him were two more cars entered for Italian regular Andrea Zanussi and for African expert Shekhar Mehta. Despite knocking a wheel off on the early spectator stages in France and dropping more than 290 places down the order, it mattered not: although both Mehta and Zanussi were waylaid with mechanical issues all three cars made the finish and the Finn, co-driven by Bernard Giroux, made an emotional return to victory.

The whole of France was entranced by this Saharan adventure, and Jean Todt wasted no opportunity to put his desert-spec cars into action. The Rallye des Pharaons was on a much more modest scale but took place in Egypt, starting and finishing in front of the majestic pyramids of Giza. Shekhar Mehta took the early lead but, having crested a dune, his 205 Turbo 16 landed badly, exactly as Vatanen's had done two years earlier, and was launched into a fierce accident that ended the popular Ugandan driver's career, while Vatanen was able to carry on and take his second desert victory.

Peugeot's senior management was not entirely convinced by the 'stretched' 205 Turbo 16, which looked too far removed from the standard road car. For 1988, therefore, new bodywork was fitted, representing the new mid-size 405 model, albeit sculpted into a coupé shape. On the 1988 Paris–Dakar, Jean Todt entered two Peugeot 205 T16 Grand Raids for Juha Kankkunen and Alain Ambrosino, together with a pair of mechanically identical Peugeot 405 T16 Grand Raids for Vatanen and French Le Mans veteran Henri Pescarolo.

By the time that the competitors reached Mali, Vatanen's lead was a little more than two hours. Then, in remarkable circumstances, a local gang stole his car and held it to ransom. The car was eventually discovered and Vatanen continued, but at this point another storm broke with the FIA over Vatanen's reinstatement and victory was credited to Juha Kankkunen and the Peugeot 205 Turbo 16.

This was to be the last major rally victory for the Peugeot 205 body shell – although the mechanical components of the Grand Raid would enjoy a hugely extended service life. The Peugeot 405 Turbo 16 Grand Raid would compete until 1990, winning two more Paris–Dakar events with Vatanen at the wheel, two more Rallye des Pharaons in 1988–89 with Vatanen and two Baja Aragón events in Spain – Vatanen in 1988 and six-time Le Mans winner Jacky Ickx in 1989.

The mechanical underpinnings of the Peugeot 205/405 Turbo 16 were then passed

ABOVE In 1988 the Peugeot 205 Turbo 16 scored an unexpected final rally victory on the Paris–Dakar when Juha Kankkunen profited from the exclusion of Ari Vatanen in the team's successor, the 405. *(McKlein)*

to Citroën's motor sport division, which was being rebuilt in the image of Jean Todt's Peugeot operation under the direction of none other than Guy Fréquelin. In 1990–94 the cars received new replacement bodies representing the Citroën ZX, maintaining PSA's stranglehold on the Sahara and desert rallying, then a heavily revised car was built for the 1994–97 seasons to try and maintain the brand's position against hugely increased competition from the Japanese manufacturers and specialist buggy constructors.

One more arena was to be conquered by the Peugeot 205 Turbo 16 in its glittering career: the Pikes Peak International Hill Climb in America. This was a huge event in the domestic racing schedule of the USA, in which competitors raced to the summit of the highest peak in the Front Range of the Rocky Mountains (but, as with most 'International' events in the USA, it was almost completely unknown across the rest of the world).

Unknown, that was, until Audi elected to go there in 1984 with Michèle Mouton and the short-wheelbase Audi Sport Quattro. Ranged against the various two-wheel-drive buggies and sprint cars that formed the bulk of the

ABOVE In 1990, PSA handed the Rally Raid programme over to sister brand Citroën, which clothed the Peugeot 205 Turbo 16 underpinnings in the body of its new ZX model, remaining at the forefront of desert events for another eight seasons. *(McKlein)*

BELOW In 1987, Peugeot almost stole the Pikes Peak International Hill Climb in America with Ari Vatanen in this hastily revamped 205 Turbo 16. *(McKlein)*

entry, the Quattro's four-wheel-drive saw it easily take the rally category and get right up among the top order, so Audi decided to make a bid for the outright win in 1985.

With a lightened and optimised Quattro at her disposal, Mouton was ready to scale the mountain. Starting at 1,500 metres above sea level, Pikes Peak rises – often through the clouds – to almost 4,500 metres at the finish line, with the cars travelling 20km along dry, loose gravel. Despite being forced to play cat and mouse with the chauvinistic sensibilities of the event organisers, Mouton took outright victory and a new course record – and Audi's marketing operation kicked into overdrive.

Audi was now big news in America and Pikes Peak became big news around the world. In 1986, in no small part to patch up the battered egos of masculine America, three-time Indianapolis 500 winner Bobby Unser fired an optimised Audi Sport Quattro S1 up the mountain to take another overall and come tantalisingly close to covering the 156-turn ascent in under 11 minutes. Then in 1987 Audi returned with a special S1 built solely for the job of setting a new all-time record in the hands of Walter Röhrl – but he was not alone.

Three bright yellow Peugeot 205 Turbo 16s were also present: one for Ari Vatanen, one for Shekhar Mehta and one for Andrea Zanussi. These cars were more mildly modified than the Audi, but had been lightened by 140kg, and were all fitted with the 1.9-litre XU9T engines that were used on the Dakar – with the power turned up to 11.

Peugeot had, in fact, been in the little Colorado town for several weeks and had rented the hill for extensive testing. Ari Vatanen had made 50 ascents by the time that the competition started, but when qualifying got underway, on his first visit and without running at full speed beforehand, he was four seconds ahead. Vatanen had a moment of crisis, wondering whether his skills had abandoned him, but Jean-Claude Vaucard and the team got to work to upgrade the standard rally aerodynamics with something a little wilder.

With a bit of jury-rigging, a second rear wing was positioned above the standard example. A new front wing was then fabricated and added on for good measure. With the 1.9-litre engine

running 3.0 bar boost its power output was raised towards 650bhp and Vatanen qualified faster than Röhrl on his final run.

Come the deciding round, Walter Röhrl pulled out another operatic fire-and-brimstone effort with the Audi's 20 valves shrieking at full stretch. Vatanen followed him and was faster, and faster again through the checkpoints but then a clamp broke on the turbo hose and he began to slow, crossing the line seven seconds behind.

For Audi it would be the last victory that fell to its mighty four-wheel-drive coupé. Peugeot would meanwhile return with the Turbo 16 bedecked in a 405 body for 1988, aerodynamically prepared for the challenge and featuring entirely new engineering that produced 800bhp and had four-wheel steering. Vatanen breezed to victory and was immortalised for Internet petrolheads the world over thanks to the award-winning short film *Climb Dance* by Jean-Louis Mourey that recorded his achievement for posterity.

Ultimately, the quality of the engineering and the calibre of the crews that were involved with the Peugeot 205 Turbo 16 created more than a decade's-worth of success in the World Rally Championship, in the major national rally series of Europe, in the Sahara and in America. It was quite simply the greatest achievement from that now-mythical Group B era.

ABOVE In 1988 a completely rebuilt car, wearing the 405 bodywork, saw Vatanen climb deeper into the affections of enthusiasts around the world with his record-breaking run at Pikes Peak captured in the movie *Climb Dance*. *(McKlein)*

Chapter Three

The Peugeot 205 Turbo 16 drivers

The rallies that the Group B supercars were designed for covered vast distances of competitive and road miles, driving both day and night for up to six days at a time. It took a certain type of person to even contemplate such a career, even in the days when the cars were built from steel on the same production lines as their showroom siblings. To do so in the cockpit of a featherweight plastic-skinned prototype like the Peugeot 205 Turbo 16 called for characters that the world simply cannot produce any longer.

OPPOSITE **With the Peugeot 205 Turbo 16 beneath them, the rally crews who drove for Peugeot Talbot Sport had plenty to smile about.** *(McKlein)*

Jean-Pierre Nicolas

If an artist was called upon to sketch the archetypal Frenchman, the result would look rather a lot like Jean-Pierre Nicolas: barrel-chested and debonair, with a shock of dark hair. If a novelist wanted to portray a French rally driver, there is little doubt that they would be born in the south of the country, where young drivers learn their skills flitting between the majestic Alps and the sun-kissed Mediterranean – and Jean-Pierre Nicolas was from Marseille.

Thus the archetypal French rally driver, known to most as JPN, cut his teeth on asphalt rallies in the mid-1960s at the wheel of a Renault 8 Gordini, following on from his father who also showed well in the 1950s and early 1960s. Most French rallies are on asphalt and JPN shone brightly enough to join the works Alpine team by the end of the decade and became synonymous with their bewitching little A110 coupés.

Thus did Nicolas play a pivotal role in many of the team's successes in the European Rally Championship, including his own most famous victory for Alpine on the 1973 Tour de Corse. That year, Corsica was also a qualifying round of the inaugural World Rally Championship for Manufacturers and JPN's victory helped Alpine etch its name in the history books as the first-ever winners of the biggest prize in rallying.

After the withdrawal of Alpine as a major factory presence, JPN moved to Peugeot, which was more at home in the rough-hewn African events than in building sleek little asphalt racers. Again, JPN thrived, showing his gravel rally skills and claiming victory on the 1976 Moroccan Rally.

His greatest year as a driver would come in 1978, when an additional World Cup was added for drivers. Without a competitive works drive for the Monte Carlo Rally, Nicolas instead took a punt on the Alméras Frères privateer Porsche team and a Group 4 911 that was fitted with a standard 3-litre road car engine.

It was a well-funded effort paid for by Gitanes tobacco and JPN convinced his old friend Jean Todt to co-drive for him, although Todt was forced to cancel at the last minute. Nicolas and the Porsche lined up against an all-star effort from both Fiat and Lancia, the sister companies each being determined to claim honours with the 131 Abarth and Stratos respectively.

What neither of the Italian factory teams had counted on was the severe snowfall that preceded the Monte that year. While the more powerful works cars slithered and skittered from one disaster to the next, JPN was able to call upon a much wider power band to smoothly head the field to the finish and claim the biggest win of his career.

Later in the season, back at Peugeot, the redoubtable Frenchman then won both of the African classics – the Safari and the Ivory Coast rallies. It was enough to see him finish second in the FIA Cup for Drivers behind winner Markku Alén.

When PSA decided to switch over to Des O'Dell's Talbot team in 1980 there seemed to be no seats for JPN to fill and so reluctantly he called time on his professional driving career. He went to work as the commercial sales director of a Renault dealership in Marseilles, which proved to be a difficult change of pace for him to live with.

So it was with no small relief that in 1982 he took a call from his old rally colleague Jean Todt, recently installed as the head of Peugeot's competition department. Todt explained that he had a groundbreaking new car that needed a good all-rounder to develop on all surfaces throughout the long months between the prototype being built and the first event. Perhaps there would even be a return to competition in a front-line car if he wanted it.

Nicolas jumped at the chance. From the moment that the Peugeot 205 T16 was

BELOW A five-time winner on the world's biggest stage, Jean-Pierre Nicolas feared that his rallying days were over until an old friend telephoned with a big idea. *(McKlein)*

unveiled, he was Todt's expert in the cockpit, both for development work and for giving updates on the car's progress to the voracious French media. And sure enough, when the car made its competition debut in the 1984 Tour de Corse, JPN was at the wheel of the second car and brought it home in a fine fourth place finish.

His Peugeot broke on the team's next outing, the Acropolis, and only one more start would be made by Nicolas in his world championship career in Sanremo, where he came home a distant fifth. It had been an enjoyable last hurrah but JPN was of a different generation to the young lions of Group B, and he was quite content to step out of the cockpit and into a managerial role.

Nicolas set about the job of managing the various national championship campaigns that Peugeot importers would embark upon through 1985–86 with the 205 Turbo 16. He did so with authority and good humour, rising up through the ranks of senior management at Peugeot Sport until, in the late 1990s, he took over as the head of the department.

At this time, Peugeot was preparing to re-enter the World Rally Championship with the 206 WRC, a car that would claim three successive manufacturers' championships in 2000–02 and drivers' titles for team leader Marcus Grönhölm in 2000 and 2002. In 2004, Peugeot's marketing team forced the WRC operation to switch to the cabriolet version of the Peugeot 307 and it fell away from potential title-winning pace, with Nicolas walking away at the end of 2005.

He was soon back in the service park, however, when Eurosport founded the Intercontinental Rally Challenge as a made-for-TV rival to the premier world series. Nicolas became the liaison man between the teams and the organisers and ultimately took the reins of the entire series in 2012, remaining at his post when the FIA restored the European Rally Championship from the IRC's organisation.

Ari Vatanen

The Vatanens were a farming family in Tuupovaara who were left shattered when, as they were travelling together, a car appeared heading straight for them on the wrong side of the road. Aarne Vatanen died at the scene

and his eight-year-old son Ari soon afterwards declared that he would master the car.

By the age of 12, Ari was driving his mother's car around the farm at breakneck speed. That summer he saw his first rally and realised that this was the only thing that he wanted to do with his life.

As he made his way into the sport, Vatanen proved unutterably brave and incredibly fast but this always meant that an accident was not far away. The crowds loved his devil-may-care approach at the wheel, but it left his team managers wondering what was going to break first – Vatanen's good fortune with injuries or their repair budgets.

In 1976 he was signed up by Ford and in the perfectly weighted Escort he found the peak of his enjoyment as a driver. Vatanen and the Escort became the great double act of British rallying, mesmerising the fans who adopted him as their own. His world

ABOVE Jean-Pierre Nicolas won three rallies on the 1978 world championship trail, his greatest being in Monte Carlo at the helm of this privateer Porsche 911. *(McKlein)*

BELOW Ari Vatanen forever won the hearts of rally fans the world over with his absolute commitment. In 1981 he got away with moments like this to be crowned world champion. *(McKlein)*

championship outings were fewer and more often ended in disaster – although, as Vatanen pointed out, from his first 101 stages at the top level, he won 10 of them.

At the end of 1980, Ford withdrew its factory team from competition until a new car to replace the venerable Escort had been built. Many of the works parts and team members moved over to David Sutton's Rothmans-backed privateer team, including Vatanen, and here he began to refine the raw speed that he had always shown with a few degrees more strategic thinking.

His first WRC win came on the Acropolis in 1980, guided by experienced Welsh co-driver Dave Richards. In 1981, Audi arrived with its technological masterpiece, the Quattro, but although lacking in outright pace on loose surfaces, the venerable Escort was bulletproof for reliability, and before long Vatanen was in contention for the drivers' world championship.

In the end it came down to the final round, the RAC Rally, which was held over stages that Vatanen knew well. Hannu Mikkola's Quattro sailed off into a distant lead but Vatanen was in sublime form and title challenger Guy Fréquelin crashed out trying to keep up, thus the title went to the Finn.

With Ford still working on its RS1700T for

Group B competition, Vatanen was forced to retreat from the world championship for much of 1982, competing in the British national championship with David Sutton and then joining the works Opel squad. He would remain with Opel in 1983 but the Manta was only an evolution of the previous Group 4 Ascona with little investment behind it to challenge the Audis or the Lancia 037.

Fortunately for Vatanen, Jean Todt was looking for a star driver to lead his new team at Peugeot. Having failed to woo double world champion Walter Röhrl or Lancia's team leader Markku Alén, he went to the Safari Rally to take another look at Vatanen, whose high-wire act did not generally sit well with the businesslike Frenchman. Fortunately for Vatanen, he delivered a supremely mature performance in Africa, pacing himself throughout the event to pounce upon victory when the Audis faltered.

In 1984, Vatanen joined Jean-Pierre Nicolas to hone the Peugeot 205 Turbo 16 through its rigorous test programme and the first competitive events of its world championship career.

He was leading handsomely on the car's debut in Corsica but crashed on the final morning, to Todt's obvious chagrin. But then came the late season start to a truly remarkable run of success, bringing mesmerising wins on the 1000 Lakes, Sanremo and RAC rallies at the end of 1984, followed by his greatest ever drive to win the 1985 Monte and then victory in Sweden a fortnight later.

Then the honeymoon ended and Vatanen found himself increasingly under pressure to stay in front of his new teammate, Timo Salonen. Salonen won three of the next four rallies and put himself into a healthy lead in the drivers' championship when the cars arrived in Argentina. Vatanen won the first stage but on the second, going flat out to protect his lead, he endured a terrifying accident.

It would be 12 weeks before Vatanen was able to get out of bed and 18 months before he was able to think about getting into a car again competitively. Aside from his physical injuries, the accident triggered a brutal depression and a form of post-traumatic stress that left him a ghostly figure, even to his own beloved family.

RIGHT Vatanen got off to a shaky start at Peugeot, crashing out of the lead on the car's debut but soon hit a golden era, winning four consecutive events. He would remain fundamental to Peugeot's successes until the 1990s.
(McKlein)

The Finn's recovery was to be inspiring. In 1987 he returned to the cockpit triumphant in Peugeot's first attempt at the Paris–Algiers–Dakar raid, following up with victories in the Rallye des Pharaons in Egypt, and he then added success in the Pikes Peak hill climb to his CV.

Vatanen also continued in rallying, although he would never again contest a full season. In 1989–90 he drove for Mitsubishi and in 1991–93 he joined Dave Richards' Prodrive team as it turned Subaru into a title contender.

He did not step out of the cockpit for good until 2006, by which time his youngest son Max was starting to show interest in rallying and Vatanen wanted to be on hand to guide him. He was also by that stage a member of the European Parliament, for which he was first elected in 1999 representing the Finnish National Coalition Party and then he was re-elected in 2004 as a member of the French Union for a Popular Movement!

Having failed to retain his seat in the 2009 European elections, Vatanen then stood as the only candidate competing with Jean Todt for the FIA presidency in 2009. Despite their long history together it was rather an ill-tempered campaign on the part of Todt's team, with

outgoing president Max Mosley more than once losing his patience with Vatanen's 'peasants' revolt' against the ordained succession.

When the voting was over, however, the two men once again joined forces, with Vatanen becoming something of an emissary on Todt's behalf, as well as taking the presidency of Estonia's national sporting body, a position which he holds to this day.

Timo Salonen

Ari Vatanen tells a very good story – one of many – about how Markku Alén went out to dinner in Helsinki not very long ago, some 25 summers after his competitive career ended, and was mobbed by his countrymen, all desperate for selfies and autographs. 'What about him? He's the world champion!' he said, pointing over their heads to the bespectacled figure standing quite contentedly out of the scrum.

That is Timo Salonen all over.

In many ways, Salonen is the more typical Finnish hero than either Vatanen or Alén. He is from the same mould as Kimi Räikkönen, someone who would do exceptional things at the wheel of a car, whether anyone was paying

ABOVE The laid-back style of Timo Salonen stood in sharp contrast to most of his peers, but when he was handed winning equipment, the Finnish hero seldom failed to deliver. *(McKlein)*

RIGHT As ever,
Salonen looks less
at ease with the
promotional side of the
job than his teammates
Michèle Mouton and
Bruno Saby before the
start of the 1986 Tour
de Corse. He preferred
to let his cars do the
talking. *(McKlein)*

attention to him or not. If the car wasn't fast
enough he would not raise the roof about it or
go bitching to the press, he simply drove it as
fast as it would go and assumed that the team
would do their bit to make it go faster next time.

Where Räikkönen's demeanour earned him
the nickname 'Iceman' among the fevered
egos of Formula 1, who thought that he was
trying to be cool, Salonen's nickname of Löysä
translates as 'slack', 'sloppy' or 'soft-boiled',
which could either refer to his less-than-
Spartan physique or to his general air of not
caring unduly about life.

Throughout most of his early career, Salonen
competed in national and regional series with
aplomb but his exposure to the potential talent
scouts of the world championship was minimal.
Only the annual 1000 Lakes gave him a chance
to take on the world's best, and usually it was
in second-rate equipment until 1977, when he
landed a seat in one of the works Fiat 131s –
and finished second.

This earned Salonen two more outings with
the Alitalia-backed team and on the next, his
first overseas outing on a rally for the Critérium
du Québec in Canada, he won by more than
four-and-a-half minutes from Simo Lampinen's
sister car. But unlike many other drivers,
victory was not the start of a fairy-tale drive to
fame and fortune. In 1979, Salonen was back
running in the Finnish series.

In fact, it was not until 1980 that Salonen
earned anything like a full-time works drive in
the world championship, and when it came
it was with Datsun. In five seasons, Salonen
contested 35 rallies and scored two wins, two
second places and 12 other points finishes.
The Datsuns were outgunned but Salonen
stuck at it, usually finishing in the top five, if the
car survived, until Jean Todt came looking for
a new number two driver to Ari Vatanen
for 1985.

Salonen seemed to offer the ideal solution.
His driving style was smooth, he was kind to
the car and he was adept at finishing the most
rough-hewn events on the calendar when other
cars broke. What nobody anticipated, least of
all Vatanen, was just how fast he would be in a
truly competitive car.

At the beginning of the season, Salonen
was not comfortable in the 205 Turbo 16;
he found the steering too weighty and it
understeered more than he liked. Once the car
was to his liking, however, he won in Portugal
and then went on a hot streak through the mid-
season run of gravel rallies to take victory in
Greece, New Zealand, Argentina and Finland
to set up a world championship double for
Peugeot in its first full season.

In 1986 it was Salonen's turn to be
impressed by the speed of a newcomer, in
the form of Juha Kankkunen. He could have

made a fuss about the new youngster with his Hollywood good looks muscling in... but it just wasn't his style. Salonen just did his best and, if it wasn't as good as Kankkunen then... he'd get him next time.

Salonen beat Kankkunen on home ground in Finland and it would be Salonen who took the 205 Turbo 16's final WRC victory in the muddy forests of Britain on the RAC Rally. It was also his last event with Peugeot Talbot Sport.

In the Group A era, Salonen spent four seasons with Mazda and two more with Mitsubishi, never once running a completely full season of events. They were not the most competitive cars of the era – that honour belonged to Lancia and Toyota – although he did take a final victory in Sweden in 1987. The 1992 Rally Portugal would mark the last competitive start of Salonen's front-line career, and having hardly occupied the spotlight in his prime he simply vanished back home to Finland to run a successful car dealership.

A decade later, Peugeot decided to honour its former champion with an outing on Finland's round of the modern WRC at the wheel of the 205 Turbo 16's successor, the 206 WRC. He started off gently, setting the 28th fastest time on the opening stage, but quietly got on with knocking the rust off and learning about his new car, rising up through the ranks to finish a creditable 14th overall.

Then he disappeared again, only resurfacing for occasional reunions such as the Eifel Rallye Festival – although, as that group of fans in Helsinki discovered, he may never be far away at all.

Juha Kankkunen

Like many of the great Scandinavian drivers, Juha Kankkunen grew up as the son of a skilled national level competitor, a member of the generation who completely turned the rallying world on its head in the 1960s.

Although the elder Kankkunen never broke through onto the international stage, the community was close-knit and when the youthful Juha showed a fierce determination to compete, his father was able to call upon expert guidance. None other than former BMC and Ford team leader Timo Makinen

helped to hone the youngster's skills before he started driving for Toyota's regional team, while making his first world championship appearances in privateer Fords and Opels.

In 1983, the 24-year-old Kankkunen was deemed ready for the international stage by Toyota chief Ove Andersson, having finished sixth on the 1000 Lakes. He retired from the Ivory Coast but scored more points on the RAC Rally, setting him up for more events in 1984, with a best finish of fifth in Finland.

The following season, Kankkunen amazed the rally world when he beat his vastly experienced former world champion teammate Björn Waldegård to win both of the classic African rallies. On both the Safari and the Ivory Coast rallies he drove with supreme confidence and impressive maturity against the acknowledged maestro of these events, but Toyota was still running a two-wheel-drive car that was down on power when compared with the Audis, Peugeots and Lancias.

If Kankkunen wanted to win more often he was going to have to fly the nest. As it happened, Jean Todt had been keeping a close eye on Kankkunen's form as he sought out a replacement for his wounded hero Ari Vatanen, and a deal was soon struck.

Fifth place in Monte Carlo was a promising start for the Finn on an event that he was not fond of. Next came Sweden and arguably his greatest ever triumph, taking on an event that has always favoured the home-grown specialists for the first time in his career, and

BELOW Juha Kankkunen remains in the very top rank of all-time greats to many rally fans. Natural skill and immense tactical awareness made him the most successful driver of his era. *(McKlein)*

becoming only the second non-Swede to win it. This was to be the first of three wins which, with three second places, handed Kankkunen the last World Rally Championship title of the Group B era after the protracted legal dispute over his team's exclusion from Sanremo.

As the Group A era got underway, Kankkunen moved to Lancia, which was the only team with a fully developed four-wheel-drive car. Team boss Cesare Fiorio tried his hardest to ensure that it would be the Italian

driver Miki Biasion who took the glory, but Kankkunen had other ideas and took his second consecutive title with victory on the season-ending RAC Rally before moving back to Toyota, where he felt more confident of the team's support.

The 1988–89 seasons were to be stymied by a multitude of retirements as the team got to grips with its ingenious Celica GT-Four. Despite disappointing WRC form, there were highlights elsewhere as Kankkunen won the Paris–Algiers–Dakar for Peugeot in 1988 and then won the Pikes Peak hill climb with Todt's team in 1989, but rallying remained his priority.

Eventually, Kankkunen lost patience with Toyota and returned to Lancia in 1990. In 1991 he was on crushing form, winning the drivers' title for a third time and notching up the highest score ever recorded by a driver, but by 1992 Toyota was faster and more reliable, and with the factory Lancias being withdrawn for 1993, Kankkunen returned home to the Japanese-owned team.

Another dominant season ensued to deliver the Finn's fourth and final drivers' title, as well as equalling the record number of 20 career rally wins in the world championship with Markku Alén. He would compete for nine more seasons, remaining with Toyota until 1997,

RIGHT Kalle Grundel (right) was insuperable for Peugeot on the German national championship, but his career with the works team effectively lasted less than a whole stage.
(McKlein)

then moving to Ford, Subaru and Hyundai. Three more rally wins came his way but the long, slow glide path out of the WRC came to an end in 2002.

In retirement, Kankkunen has largely stayed out of the limelight, with his most regular activities being focused on running an ice driving centre after the collapse of a domestic airline, Flying Finn, in which he was an investor. In 2010, he was invited to take part in the 60th anniversary running of the Rally Finland at the wheel of a second-string Ford Focus, in which he finished eighth in front of many series regulars.

And the Irregulars...

Peugeot Talbot Sport was not a large organisation by modern standards, nor even when compared with those of Audi or Lancia. Its testing and development programme of 1983 was done with one driver, increasing to two drivers during 1984 and the start of Peugeot's competitive story with the 205 Turbo 16.

At the start of the 1985 season, a third car was added, for which the 1981 French champion and long-time Renault driver Bruno Saby was brought into the fold. Manufacturer racing teams have always been unapologetically nationalistic and having a French driver at Peugeot was no more important than having a German at Audi, an Italian at Lancia or a Briton at Austin Rover.

Saby was popular, marketable and would drive with gusto at every opportunity. That was enough, so provided that the big guns from Scandinavia were delivering the wins and titles, having a Frenchman in the supporting role, picking up manufacturer points would always play well.

It would always be hard to bet on a 'home-grown' driver beating the Scandinavians on equal terms, however. The simple fact was that the domestic sport in France, from which any future stars emerged, was primarily based on closed public roads, in just the same way as the Scandinavians and Brits grew up rallying on forest tracks.

Saby was kept fully occupied as the anchor for the E2 testing programme, while his greatest moment came on one of the darkest weekends in world championship history, on the 1986 Tour de Corse. He had been leading the pursuit of Henri Toivonen's Lancia throughout the early stages, and enjoyed enough of a gap to the next car, François Chatriot's Renault, that he simply had to drive through the final day to take a joyless but valuable win.

In the wake of Vatanen's accident on the 1985 Argentina Rally, Jean Todt needed to find a suitable replacement to fill in on the rest of the world championship rounds. His first thought was to look in-house at the various 205 Turbo 16 programmes being run by Peugeot's national importers, of which far and away the most important – and the most successful – was in Germany.

Swedish driver Kalle Grundel was all-but unbeatable on German national events in 1985, and had previously been the star of the Group A production-based class for Volkswagen, powering a Golf GTI up in among the four-wheel-drive supercars of Group B.

His form did not carry over to the senior category, however. Called up to deputise for Vatanen and told that he need only finish sixth to assure Peugeot of the manufacturers' title, he went off on the first stage. Although the car made it out of the stage for the team to weld its broken suspension mounts, and would eventually finish fifth, Todt had seen enough.

Another Group A star that Peugeot signed up for a national programme was Mikael Sundström, who joined Des O'Dell's UK operation and drove both Group A and Group B machinery. He was in the mould of Ari Vatanen – faster than fast but prone to hurling his car at the scenery. He had one outing for the works team on the 1986 RAC Rally, winning two stages on his way to finishing in fourth place behind Salonen, Alén and Kankkunen.

Sundström went on to spend the next five years with Mazda in national, European and world championship events. He either won or crashed, and when Mazda scaled down its operations he tried his luck in a production class Lancia Delta Integrale without success. There would be one last victory in a Mazda on the 1993 Arctic Rally but then Sundström was forced out of the sport and he died in 1999 due to health problems brought on by alcohol addiction.

The other major national rally programme was in Italy, run by the Alméras Frères team that had previously been the leading specialist in Porsche rally cars. Its first season in 1985 was a disappointment, in which long-term Talbot driver Giovanni del Zoppo was rather out of his depth, stepping up from the tiny front-wheel-drive Talbot Samba to try and master the Peugeot 205 Turbo 16.

For 1986, the team splashed out on Lancia driver Andrea Zanussi, who was a safe pair of hands with a strong finishing record and seven wins at European championship level. He completely demolished the field through his

single season in the Peugeot 205 Turbo 16, starting eleven rallies and winning five of them, with two second places, one third and one fourth. He would remain with Peugeot Sport through its adventures on the Dakar and Pikes Peak, before stepping away from full-time competition in 1991.

Before Group B, Peugeot's production-based cars were always among the favourites in Africa's gruelling road rallies, soaking up enormous punishment and covering colossal distances with apparent ease. When Jean Todt and the Peugeot 205 Turbo 16s first went on the Safari Rally in 1985 they were shaken apart and only Timo Salonen could coax what remained of his car to the finish.

French honour had to be restored in Africa and to this end Todt hired the most experienced driver on the continent, Shekhar Mehta, to lead an intensive programme of testing and development. The result was a huge step forward, and when the Group B era ended it was Mehta who was involved in getting the team ready by adapting these 'Safari-spec' cars for the Paris-Alger-Dakar marathon.

The Uganda-born driver was leading on the 1987 Rallye des Pharaons in Egypt when he suffered a similar accident to Vatanen's in Argentina. He was flown to Paris for treatment on cracked vertebrae, broken ribs, extensive internal injuries and a life-threatening infection, but eventually pulled through. He retired from competition and joined the FIA's rallies commission, heading the department from 1997 until 2005 and was then reinstated in 2006 when his health, still affected by the 1987 crash, rapidly deteriorated and he died in a London hospital.

In late 1985, Audi Sport had a major shake-up of its staff and operations. It was clear that the team's idea of keeping its Group B cars based on a production shell and powertrain were never going to keep pace with the purpose-built mid-engined cars and the more power that they threw at the Quattros, the harder they became to control.

Team boss Roland Gumpert was moved on and with him went the 1982 championship runner-up Michèle Mouton. Todt had considered her as a candidate for Peugeot Talbot Sport from the outset, but feared that the

LEFT African sporting legend Shekhar Mehta was a five-time Safari Rally winner who led the development of the 'Safari-spec' 205 Turbo 16 and drove in both Peugeot's Rally Raid and Pike's Peak programmes. *(McKlein)*

weight of publicity and expectation for having the only woman to have succeeded at the top level (never mind the only *Frenchwoman* to have done so), would turn his efficient team into a three-ring circus.

By 1986, Mouton had spent considerable time on the substitute's bench at Audi and there was considerably less pressure on her. She signed a deal to replace Kalle Grundel in the German championship on the proviso that she got to compete in her favourite world championship events, and thus duly appeared at the wheel of a first-generation car on the Monte Carlo Rally with Terry Harryman alongside her.

Her Monte Carlo ended early with a rare mechanical failure for the 205 Turbo 16, but her German campaign was flawless, winning six out of nine events and claiming the title at a canter. Her only other outing would come in Corsica as a full works driver, this time reunited with her long-time co-driver at Audi, Fabrizia Pons. It would be a sad finale to Mouton's WRC career, going out with gearbox failure early on and then standing by helpless as her good friend Henri Toivonen and his co-driver Sergio Cresto perished.

The car that Mouton drove in Corsica, chassis C207, later reappeared on the 1000 Lakes in the hands of another Audi refugee: 1984 world champion, Stig Blomqvist. Jean Todt had taken the Swede's decision to leave Talbot for Audi in 1982 rather personally, but the rally community is small and wounds tend to get healed quickly.

After leaving Audi at the end of 1985, Blomqvist had moved to Ford, becoming its team leader as the RS200 was finally being prepared for competition. Barely had the team got into its stride, however, before Portugal happened, when an RS200 went into the crowd.

Then Corsica happened and Group B's future hung by a thread; then came the Hessen Rally in Germany, in which F1 star Marc Surer hit a tree in an RS200 which broke in half and exploded, killing his co-driver Michel Wyder. Group B was finished at that point, and with it the RS200 programme, so when Jean Todt needed an extra driver to help fend off Lancia late in the season, Ford was happy to release him.

In his two starts with Peugeot, Blomqvist finished third in Argentina with two stage wins, the only 205 Turbo 16 still running at the finish. Then he took fourth in Finland, with four stage wins, and prevented more than one Lancia getting into the top four finishers. It was exactly the sort of professional job that Todt had always wanted from whoever took the wheel of his fabulous creation.

Chapter Four

Anatomy of the Peugeot 205 Turbo 16

Every single car that has ever been designed, whether for road use, competition use or bouncing over the lunar landscape is essentially a three-dimensional collection of compromises. The achievements of the Peugeot 205 Turbo 16 came from mastering the balance of form and function in the most exacting environment.

OPPOSITE The design of the Peugeot 205 Turbo 16 balanced form and function. It had to deliver shattering performance, be easy for mechanics to work on in the field (or in the forest, or the desert...) and it had to look like the regular 205 supermini. *(Author)*

Peugeot 205 Turbo 16 chassis histories

The history of any individual competition car and its components is often hard to trace, but this is more often true in rallying than in any other branch of the sport. The case of the Peugeot 205 Turbo 16 is acute because so many cars were later repurposed to compete again in different forms of competition. As 1986 world champion Juha Kankkunen put it: 'I know that my car in my collection is the one I won with in Sweden the first time I went there. Any of the others... maybe not so much!'

Chassis	Type	Registration	Event	Crew	Result	Notes
C1	Peugeot 205 Turbo 16	323 EXA 75	1984 Tour de Corse	Vatanen / Harryman	Rtd (accident)	Written off after fire burnt the car out
C2	Peugeot 205 Turbo 16	697 EXC 75	1984 Tour de Corse	Nicolas / Charley	4th	Written off by a mechanic before the start of 1985 Safari
			1985 Safari	Saby / Fauchille	DNS	
C3	Peugeot 205 Turbo 16	716 EXC 75	1984 Acropolis	Vatanen / Harryman	Rtd (engine)	Written off after fire burnt the car out
C4	Peugeot 205 Turbo 16	709 EXC 75	1984 1000 Lakes	Vatanen / Harryman	1st	In private ownership
			1984 Acropolis	Nicolas / Charley	Rtd (driveshaft)	
C5	Peugeot 205 Turbo 16	704 EXC 75	1984 Sanremo	Vatanen / Harryman	Recce car	In private ownership
			1985 Monte Carlo	Salonen / Harjanne	Recce car	
			1985 Portugal	Vatanen / Harryman	Recce car	
			1985 Tour de Corse	Salonen / Harjanne	Recce car	
C6	Peugeot 205 Turbo 16	123 FBL 75	1985 Portugal	Salonen / Harjanne	Recce car	In private ownership
			1985 Tour de Corse	Saby / Fauchille	Recce car	
			1985 Acropolis	Salonen / Harjanne	Recce car	
C7	Peugeot 205 Turbo 16	128 FBL 75	1985 Sanremo	Vatanen / Harryman	1st	Unknown thereafter
			1985 RAC	Vatanen / Harryman	1st	
C8	Peugeot 205 Turbo 16	123 FBL 75	1985 Monte Carlo	Saby / Fauchille	5th	In private ownership
			1985 Safari	Salonen / Harjanne	7th	
C9	Peugeot 205 Turbo 16	704 EXC 75	1985 Safari	Vatanen / Harryman	Rtd (head gasket)	Owned by Peugeot, displayed at the Schlumpf Museum
C10	Peugeot 205 Turbo 16	323 EXA 75	1985 Monte Carlo	Salonen / Harjanne	3rd	Unknown thereafter
			1985 Swedish	Salonen / Harjanne	3rd	
		25 FGV 75	1985 Tour de Corse	Salonen / Harjanne	Rtd (electrical)	
			1985 Acropolis	Salonen / Harjanne	1st	
C11	Peugeot 205 Turbo 16	716 EXC 75	1985 Monte Carlo	Vatanen / Harryman	1st	Auctioned by RM Sotheby's at 2016 Rétromobile
			1985 Swedish	Vatanen / Harryman	1st	
			1985 Portugal	Vatanen / Harryman	Rtd (engine)	
			1985 Tour de Corse	Vatanen / Harryman	Recce car	
			1985 Acropolis	Vatanen / Harryman	Recce car	
			1986 Sanremo	Vatanen / Harryman	Recce car	

Chassis	Type	Registration	Event	Crew	Result	Notes
C12	Peugeot 205 Turbo 16	323 EXA 75	1985 Portugal	Salonen / Harjanne	1st	Unknown thereafter
			1985 Safari	Saby / Fauchille	Rtd (accident)	
C13	Peugeot 205 Turbo 16	SB-K 205	1985 Sachs Winter Rally	Grundel / Diekmann	1st	Believed to have been written off in Germany. An authentic replica has been built using a 205 Turbo 16 road car
			1985 Saarland Rally	Grundel / Diekmann	1st	
			1985 Metz Rally	Grundel / Diekmann	Rtd	
			1985 Vorderpfalz Rally	Grundel / Diekmann	1st	
			1985 Rally Hessen	Grundel / Diekmann	1st	
			1985 Hunsrück Rally	Grundel / Diekmann	1st	
			1985 Heidelberg Rally	Grundel / Diekmann	1st	
			1985 Rally Deutschland	Grundel / Diekmann	1st	
			1985 Baltic Rally	Grundel / Diekmann	1st	
			1985 3-Städte Rally	Grundel / Diekmann	1st	
			1986 Monte Carlo	Mouton / Harryman	Rtd (engine)	
			1986 Sachs Winter Rally	Mouton / Harryman	Rtd (accident)	
			1986 Rally Kohle & Stahl	Mouton / Harryman	1st	
			1986 Vorderpfalz Rally	Mouton / Harryman	1st	
			1986 Rally Hessen	Mouton / Harryman	1st	
			1986 Ypres 24 Hours	Saby / Fauchille	Rtd (accident)	
			1986 Hunsrück Rally	Mouton / Harryman	Rtd (turbo)	
			1986 Rally Deutschland	Mouton / Harryman	1st	
			1986 Baltic Rally	Mouton / Harryman	1st	
			1986 3-Städte Rally	Mouton / Harryman	1st	
C14	Peugeot 205 Turbo 16	25 TC 34	1985 Rally Costa Brava	Zanini / Autet	Rtd (accident)	Operated by Alméras brothers' team for Peugeot Spain
			1985 Rally Costa Blanca	Zanini / Autet	6th	
			1985 Rally Girona	Zanini / Autet	Rtd (accident)	
			1985 Rally Villa de Llanes	Saby / Fauchille	1st	
			1985 Rally Corte Ingles	Saby / Fauchille	Rtd (oil pressure)	
		VD700004	1986 Criterium Jurassien	Oguey / Remy	4th	
		VD700027	1986 Rally Geneva	Oguey / Remy	1st	
			1986 Elba Rally	Oguey / Remy	7th	
			1986 Lugano Rally	Oguey / Remy	3rd	
			1986 Rally della Lana	Oguey / Remy	Rtd (accident)	
		VD700025	1986 Rally Baden-Württemberg	Oguey / Remy	3rd	
			1986 Rally de Court	Oguey / Remy	1st	
		VD700026	1986 Rally du Valais	Oguey / Remy	2nd	
C15	Peugeot 205 Turbo 16	MI 64170X	1985 1000 Miglia	del Zoppo / Tognana	2nd	In private ownership
			1985 Costa Smeralda	del Zoppo / Tognana	Rtd (engine)	
			1985 Elba Rally	del Zoppo / Tognana	Rtd (engine)	
			1985 Sassari	del Zoppo / Tognana	1st	
			1985 Targa Florio	del Zoppo / Tognana	Rtd (accident)	
			1985 della Lana	del Zoppo / Tognana	Rtd (engine)	
			1985 Piancavallo	del Zoppo / Tognana	Rtd (electrical)	
			1985 Sanremo	del Zoppo / Tognana	7th	
			1986 1000 Miglia	Zanussi / Amati	4th	
			1986 Costa Smeralda	Zanussi / Amati	2nd	
			1986 Elba Rally	Zanussi / Amati	3rd	
			1986 Lanterna	Zanussi / Amati	1st	
			1986 Targa Florio	Zanussi / Amati	2nd	
			1986 Piemonte	Zanussi / Amati	1st	
C16	Peugeot 205 Turbo 16	26 FGV 75	1985 Tour de Corse	Vatanen / Harryman	Rtd (accident)	Written off in 80-foot drop off a hillside
C17	Peugeot 205 Turbo 16	26 FGV 75	1985 Acropolis	Vatanen / Harryman	Rtd (steering)	Auctioned by Artcurial at 2014 Rétromobile, sold for €274,160. At the time of writing for sale in the UK through Jeremy Cottingham.
		709 EXC 75	1985 Argentina	Reutemann / Fauchille	3rd	
C18	Peugeot 205 Turbo 16	704 EXC 75	1985 New Zealand	Salonen / Harjanne	1st	On display at l'Aventure Peugeot
			1985 Argentina	Salonen / Harjanne	1st	

Chassis	Type	Registration	Event	Crew	Result	Notes
C19	Peugeot 205 Turbo 16	123 FBL 75	1985 New Zealand	Vatanen / Harryman	2nd	Written off in Argentina
			1985 Argentina	Vatanen / Harryman	Rtd (accident)	
C20	Peugeot 205 Turbo 16	B555 SRW	1985 Scottish	Sundström / White	Rtd (accident)	Operated by Des O'Dell/Talbot team. Retained by Peugeot UK, displayed at the Coventry Transport Museum
			1985 Ulster	Sundström / White	3rd	
			1985 Manx	Sundström / White	Rtd (engine)	
			1985 RAC	Sundström / White	Rtd (accident)	
			1986 National Breakdown	Sundström / Silander	Rtd (accident)	
			1986 Circuit of Ireland	Sundström / Silander	Rtd (clutch)	
			1986 Welsh International	Sundström / Silander	Rtd (OTL)	
			1986 Scottish	Sundström / Silander	1st	
			1986 Lurgan Park	Sundström / Silander	1st	
			1986 Ulster	Sundström / Silander	3rd	
			1986 Manx	Sundström / Silander	4th	
M1	Peugeot 205 Turbo 16	243 EVZ 75	1984 Tour de Corse	Nicolas / Charley	Recce car	Ex-works car rebuilt for Darniche. Restored to Gauloises livery from the 1985 Tour de Corse by F.A. Automobile and sold to a private owner
			1984 Acropolis	Nicolas / Charley	Recce car	
			1985 Monte Carlo	Saby / Fauchille	Recce car	
			1985 Swedish	Salonen / Harjanne	Recce car	
		932 SB 74	1985 Tour de Corse	Darniche / Mahé	Rtd (fuel pump)	
			1985 Ypres 24 Hours	Darniche / Mahé	Rtd (differential)	
			1985 Tour de la Réunion	Darniche / Mahé	Rtd (accident)	
			1986 Rally du Valais	Darniche / Mahé	Rtd (accident)	
P4	Peugeot 205 Turbo 16	974 ESZ 75	1984 Tour de Corse	Vatanen / Harryman	Recce car	In private ownership, believed fitted with a Pikes Peak engine.
			1984 Acropolis	Vatanen / Harryman	Recce car	
P200	Peugeot 205 Turbo 16		1985 Sanremo	Salonen / Harjanne	Recce car	Prototype E2 specification test car
S7	Peugeot 205 Turbo 16	987 771				In private ownership
S14	Peugeot 205 Turbo 16					In private ownership, converted to E2 specification
S36	Peugeot 205 Turbo 16	284 FVF 75	1986 Terre Provence	Ballet / Lallement	Rtd (clutch)	In private ownership
			1986 Ronde Découverte	Ballet / Lallement	1st	
			1986 Terre de Charente	Ballet / Lallement	Rtd (transmission)	
			1986 1000 Pistes	Ballet / Lallement	2nd	
			1986 Tour de la Réunion	Ballet / Lallement	1st	
			1986 Ronde des Terres de Beauce	Ballet / Lallement	Rtd (accident)	
			1986 Terre de Castine	Ballet / Lallement	1st	
			1986 Terre de Valbonne	Ballet / Lallement	Rtd (puncture)	
			1986 Terre de Cardabelles	Ballet / Lallement	1st	
			1986 Criterium des Cévennes	Ballet / Lallement	7th	
N/A	Peugeot 205 Turbo 16	YN.482	1985 Suikerstreek	Gewent / Frank	38th	Road car with 300 bhp competition pack
			1985 Midden-Limberg	Gewent / Pranuck	3rd	
			1985 Limburgia	Gewent	Course Car	
			1985 Leuven	Gewent / Claes	2nd	
			1985 Pepijnrally	Gewent / Claes	3rd	
			1985 Grensland	Gewent / Claes	Rtd	
			1985 Boucles Liège	Gewent / Claes	Rtd	
			1986 van Mechelen	Gewent / Claes	Rtd	
			1986 Kempenrally	Gewent / Claes	Rtd	
			1986 Rallye de Hannut	Gewent / Jacobs	8th	
			1986 Houtland	Gewent / Claes	7th	
			1986 TAC Rally	Gewent / Claes	4th	
			1986 12 Heures de March	Gewent / Claes	Rtd	
			1986 Ypres 24 Hours	Gewent / Jacobs	Rtd	
			1986 Limburgia	Gewent / Clauwert	9th	
			1986 van Leuven	Gewent / Clauwert	7th	
			1986 van Looi	Gewent / Clauwert	Rtd (differential)	
			1986 d'Aubel	Gewent / Clauwert	Rtd (transmission)	
			1986 Boucles de Liège	Gewent / Clauwert	Rtd (differential)	

Chassis	Type	Registration	Event	Crew	Result	Notes
N/A	Peugeot 205 Turbo 16	205 PM 59	1986 Béthunois	Ivens	Course Car	Road car with 300 bhp competition pack
			1986 Cédico	Ivens / Mace	1st	
			1986 du Touquet	Ivens / Mace	1st	
			1986 Ypres 24 Hours	Ivens / Mace	Rtd	
			1986 Tour de la Réunion	Ivens	Rtd (clutch)	
			1987 National du Nord	Ivens	Course Car	
6000 RB 78	Peugeot 205 Turbo 16	6000 RB 78	1984 Tour de France	Joyes / Fontaine	Rtd	Road car with 300 bhp competition pack
		5173 TB 42	1985 Monte Carlo	Gardère / Bufferne	12th	
			1985 Tour de Corse	Gardère / Bufferne	Rtd	
			1985 du Forez	Gardère / Bufferne	Rtd	
			1986 Monte Carlo	Gardère / Bufferne	Rtd	
			1986 Swedish	Gardère / Bufferne	20th	
			1986 Tour de Corse	Gardère / Bufferne	Rtd	
C201	Peugeot 205 Turbo 16 E2	24 FGV 75	1985 Tour de Corse	Saby / Fauchille	2nd	Owned by the Loheac Museum
			1985 Bettega Memorial	Salonen	1st	
C202	Peugeot 205 Turbo 16 E2	704 EXC 75	1985 1000 Lakes	Salonen / Harjanne	1st	Unknown thereafter
C203	Peugeot 205 Turbo 16 E2	709 EXC 75	1985 1000 Lakes	Grundel / Diekmann	5th	Unknown thereafter
C204	Peugeot 205 Turbo 16 E2	704 EXC 75	1985 Sanremo	Salonen / Harjanne	2nd	In private ownership
			1985 RAC	Salonen / Harjanne	Rtd (oil pressure)	
C205	Peugeot 205 Turbo 16 E2	709 EXC 75	1985 Sanremo	Saby / Fauchille	Rtd (engine)	Unknown thereafter
			1985 RAC	Grundel / Harryman	Rtd (accident)	
C206	Peugeot 205 Turbo 16 E2	24 FGV 75	1986 Monte Carlo	Salonen / Harjanne	2nd	Unknown thereafter
		311 FPF 75	1986 Acropolis	Salonen / Harjanne	Rtd (suspension)	
			1986 Sanremo	Vatanen / Harryman	Course Car	
C207	Peugeot 205 Turbo 16 E2	25 FGV 75	1986 Monte Carlo	Kankkunen / Piironen	5th	In private ownership
		244 FWH 75	1986 Tour de Corse	Mouton / Pons	Rtd (transmission)	
		319 FPF 75	1986 Acropolis	Kankkunen / Piironen	1st	
			1986 Argentina	Kankkunen / Piironen	Rtd (suspension)	
			1986 Sanremo	Kankkunen / Piironen	DSQ	
			1986 RAC	Salonen / Harjanne	1st	
C208	Peugeot 205 Turbo 16 E2	26 FGV 75	1986 Monte Carlo	Saby / Fauchille	6th	Owned by Juha Kankkunen
			1986 Swedish	Kankkunen / Piironen	1st	
			1986 Tour de Corse	Kankkunen / Piironen	Withdrawn	
C209	Peugeot 205 Turbo 16 E2	709 EXC 75	1986 Swedish	Salonen / Harjanne	Rtd (oil pressure)	European Rallycross Championship winner 1988–90 with Matti Alamäki, owned by the Loheac Manoir de l'Automobile
C210	Peugeot 205 Turbo 16 E2	311 FPF 75	1986 Portugal	Salonen / Harjanne	Withdrawn	In private ownership
		239 FWH 75	1986 1000 Lakes	Kankkunen / Piironen	2nd	
			1986 Sanremo	Saby / Fauchille	DSQ	
			1986 Valle d'Aosta	Saby / Fauchille	2nd	
C211	Peugeot 205 Turbo 16 E2	287 FPF 75	1986 Safari	Kankkunen / Piironen	5th	Ari Vatanen 1987 Pikes Peak car, later converted to 405 T16 Pikes Peak. Retained by Peugeot
		237 FWH 75	1986 1000 Lakes	Salonen / Harjanne	1st	
			1986 Sanremo	Salonen / Harjanne	Rtd (accident)	
			1986 RAC	Kankkunen / Piironen	3rd	
C212	Peugeot 205 Turbo 16 E2	290 FPF 75	1986 Safari	Mehta / Combes	8th	Andrea Zanussi 1987 Pikes Peak car, subsequently converted to Peugeot 405 T16. In private ownership
		244 FWH 75	1986 Acropolis	Saby / Fauchille	3rd	
			1986 Argentina	Saby / Fauchille	Rtd (engine)	
			1986 1000 Lakes	Blomqvist / Berglund	4th	
C213	Peugeot 205 Turbo 16 E2	237 FWH 75	1986 Tour de Corse	Salonen / Harjanne	Rtd (accident)	In private ownership, restored to represent the Kankkunen / Piironen 1985 Safari car
		287 FPF 75	1986 RAC	Sundström / Silander	4th	
C214	Peugeot 205 Turbo 16 E2	239 FWH 75	1986 Tour de Corse	Saby / Fauchille	1st	1987 Pikes Peak car, converted to 405 T16 Pikes Peak spec. Retained by Peugeot
		294 FPF 75	1986 Olympus	Kankkunen / Piironen	2nd	
C215						Converted to Grand Raid specification
C216	Peugeot 205 Turbo 16 E2	319 FPF 75	1986 New Zealand	Kankkunen / Piironen	1st	In private ownership
		311 FPF 75	1986 Argentina	Blomqvist / Berglund	3rd	
C217	Peugeot 205 Turbo 16 E2	311 FPF 75	1986 New Zealand	Salonen / Harjanne	5th	Converted to Grand Raid specification
C218	Peugeot 205 Turbo 16 E2					Rallycross car 1988–89. Believed stolen
C219	Peugeot 205 Turbo 16 E2					Converted to Grand Raid specification
C230	Peugeot 205 Turbo 16 E2					Converted to Grand Raid specification

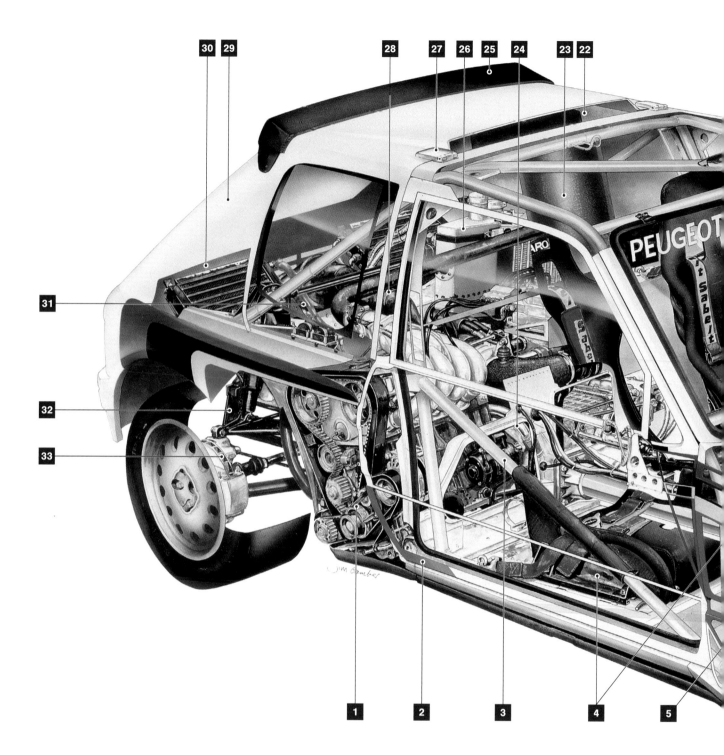

Peugeot 205 T16 in tarmac specification.

(Bamber family archive)

1 Peugeot XU8T engine
2 Central monocoque
3 Integral rollcage
4 Fuel tanks
5 Plastic body mouding

6 Asphalt tyre
7 15in competition wheel
8 Fire extinguisher
9 300mm single-caliper disc brake
10 Front shock absorber/coil spring assembly
11 Front subframe assembly
12 Wishbone suspension
13 Front differential
14 Front driveshaft

15 Cooling fan
16 Towing hook
17 Spare wheel
18 Fuel filler neck
19 Hydraulic fluid reservoirs
20 Gear lever
21 Handbrake
22 Air intake
23 Oil tank
24 Gearbox
25 Rear wing

26 Engine management system ECU
27 Rear bodywork hinges
28 Turbocharger
29 Unitary plastic rear body moulding
30 Oil cooler
31 Ignition HT leads
32 Rear subframe assembly
33 273mm single caliper disk brake

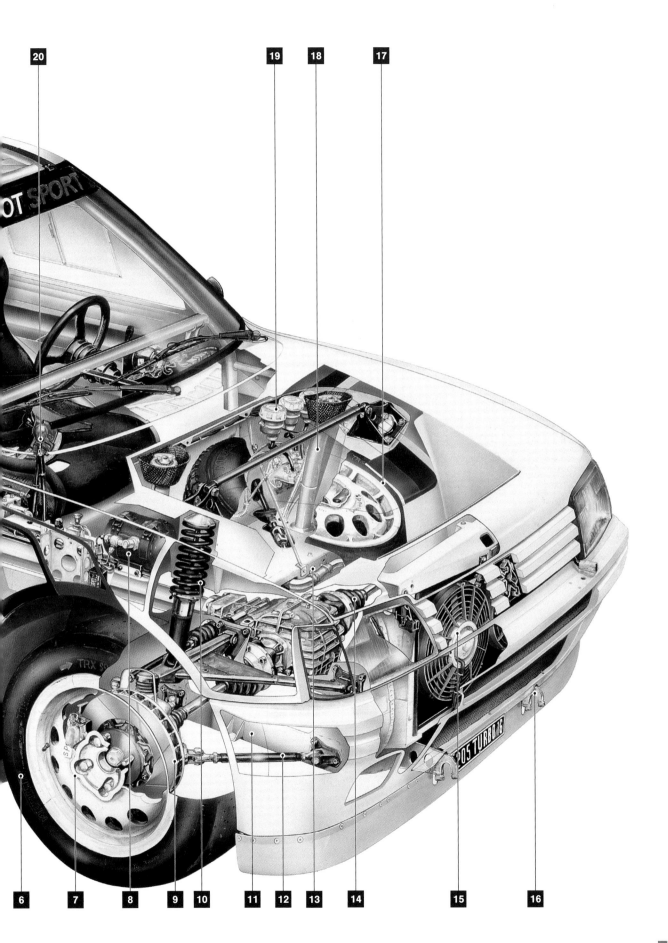

20 **19** **18** **17**

6 **7** **8** **9** **10** **11** **12** **13** **14** **15** **16**

In component form the Peugeot 205 Turbo 16 looks so simple and logical that anyone could build it.
(Getty Images)

Body, chassis and aerodynamics

When the Peugeot 205 Turbo 16 was conceived and it still carried the 'M24 Rallye' nameplate on its designs, the bodywork was of significantly less influence than the fundamental structure of the car. Group B allowed engineers almost total freedom to build whatever they wanted beneath the skin, but it was the three decades of experience in engineering sports-prototype, GT and rally cars that lay within the ebullient Des O'Dell that laid out the fundamental architecture of the car.

With his long years of fixing cars in the middle of the night at Le Mans or in the forests, O'Dell knew that the first requirement of the car was to be as user-friendly to the engineers as possible. The structure could be as light as a feather and stronger than granite, but if the mechanics couldn't access the main parts that were likely to cause delays and retirements then it would be useless.

The road-going Peugeot 205 donated the central monocoque in which the crew would sit, together with the correct-sized windscreen angled in the perpendicular manner of a regular hatchback. Unlike aerodynamically honed circuit racers, this is no disadvantage in a rally car because a more vertical screen helps to cut out unwanted glare and give the driver a better sense of where the front corners are.

When Audi chose to shorten the wheelbase of its all-conquering Quattro, the opportunity was also grabbed to swap the steeply raked windscreen and A-pillars of the coupé for the more upright setup from the Audi 80 on which it was based. Even Ford, with its purpose-built RS200, chose to use the front windscreen and pillars from the Ford Sierra for this same reason.

As far as the chassis and body design of the Peugeot 205 Turbo 16 was concerned, the central compartment was effectively a sealed unit. The standard car was cut off level with the trailing edge of the door and a sturdy firewall sealed the occupants in. What sat fore and aft of the crew's quarters was where the designers and engineers would earn their keep.

The biggest question was the location of the engine. Following conventional wisdom, O'Dell at first pushed for the mid-mounted engine to sit

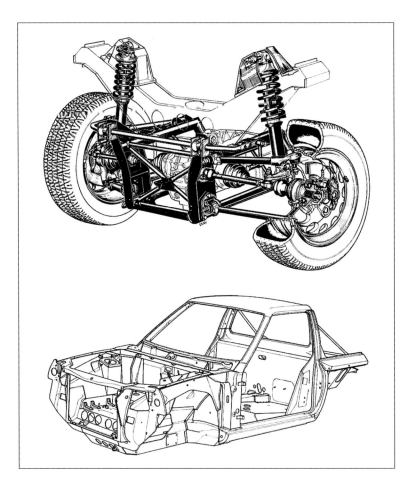

ABOVE The basic structure of the road car and first competition cars laid bare: a central monocoque from the road car with large pressings to anchor the rest of the structure. Front and rear suspension and transmissions sat in identical subframes. *(Peugeot)*

BELOW Peugeot Talbot Sport engineers assemble one of the prototype cars in 1983, revealing the fuel tanks located beneath each seat, firewall and subframes. *(McKlein)*

longitudinally in the car as it did on the Lancia 037 (and practically every successful circuit racing car). By choosing the relatively small four-cylinder XU engine and a turbocharger, however, routing all of the ancillaries and finding space for the transmission within the confines of the Peugeot 205 shell meant that it would have to be mounted transversely as close to the centre of the car as possible.

Seating the engine transversely would also mean that there were no driveshafts or propshafts running beneath it, lowering the car's centre. The choice of gearbox also meant that running east–west was always going to be the best compromise.

Another compromise on the layout was that Peugeot was going to have to build and sell 200 road-going versions of the car, and that this would place very different demands on the weight distribution. It was imagined that most journeys would be made by the driver alone and that they would be sitting on the left, which meant that the greater mass of the engine would have to sit on the right.

To help with weight distribution and access, the engine was tilted backwards by 20 degrees and biased heavily to the right-hand side of the car. This enabled comparatively compact exterior dimensions to follow the form of the 205 road car. Both

ABOVE The transverse arrangement of the engine and gearbox, located roughly where the rear footwell would be in a regular 205, was unique among Group B rally cars and dictated much of the structural design. *(Peugeot)*

CENTRE With the access panels back in place, the bodywork retained a remarkably unified look while protecting the most vulnerable components. *(Author)*

RIGHT When the car was fully assembled, its engine and transmission were buried beneath the ancillaries in an incredibly crowded workspace for the mechanics. *(Author)*

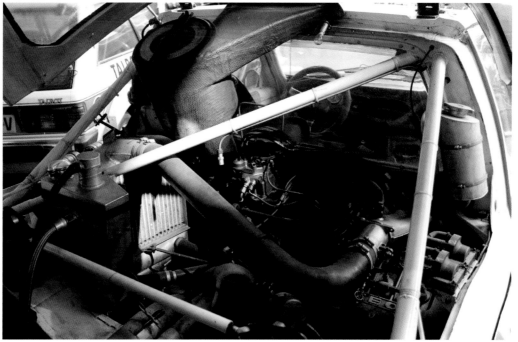

the engine and transmission were held in place – effectively replacing the rear seats – by a stout spaceframe that featured, on the first evolution of the design, two girder-like longitudinal pressings around which the rest of the structure and roll cage were then fitted.

Most of the ancillaries for the engine were then placed on top of the gearbox to try and balance up the weight distribution and maintain the easiest access possible for hard-pressed mechanics on event. On either side of its outer shell, the car featured removable panels in front of the rear wheel arch through which on the right-hand side it was easy to access the belts on the engine's front face. The left-hand panel gave immediate access to the torque-splitting equipment and viscous coupling centre differential which sat on the exposed face of the gearbox.

The ignition and electrics were lifted as high as possible out of the firing line from stones, dust and water ingress that would be part-and-parcel of a rally car's life. On the road cars and the initial batch of 20 'Evolution' rally cars that would contest the 1984–85 World Rally Championship seasons, the oil coolers, oil tank and heat exchangers were all pushed to the rear.

The primary fuel tanks sat amidships directly beneath the driver and co-driver's seats. On the pre-production test car, the seats had to be removed to top up the tanks but on the production run the filler caps were routed through the front firewall to sit roughly where the windscreen washer filler would be on the regular car.

Forward of the windscreen, the basic shape of the engine bay was retained but the largest item in there by far was the spare wheel and tool kit. The master cylinders for the hydraulics sat mounted on the firewall and there was the radiator and fan arrangement up in the nose, while the rest of the metalwork was pared to the bone... quite what modern crash-testing might reveal about the integrity of mid-engined Group B cars doesn't bear thinking about.

RIGHT The body panels were made of plastic and the structure was pure competition car, but Peugeot managed to ensure that to the casual observer the rally car was pure 205. (Author)

LEFT The firewall enclosed the monocoque centre section, with the Perspex screen giving at least some concession to rearward vision. (Author)

LEFT The roll cage ran through the full length of the car and was integrated within the original steel of the remaining 205 road car structure. By modern standards it looks insubstantial, but its performance was well tested in service. (Author)

It was another of Des O'Dell's dicta that the suspension, both front and rear, should be mounted on their own subframes and that the design and fit of these structures should be completely interchangeable, to help with both costs and usability. These cradles would hold the front and rear differentials and the mounting points for the upper and lower wishbones upon which the springs and dampers could then be attached.

The bodywork that clothed this skeleton was made from plastics rather than carbon fibre as it would be today. It was styled by the same team that had produced the 205 road car with input from the racing engineers, with the objective of looking as close as possible to even the humblest 954cc GL.

Access was of paramount importance, which is why the entire rear section of the car lifted up, hinged at the top of the firewall behind the driver and co-driver's seats. At the front, the bonnet looked roughly proportional to the road car's but its design was dominated by the scoop that plunged down behind the front-mounted radiator to allow hot air to escape up and over the car's exterior.

Production of these front and rear panels, as well as the plastic front wings, doors and access hatches for the engine and gearbox

ABOVE Coachbuilder Heuliez created all of the panels for the competition cars and the road cars alike. Rather than taking a road car and making a competition vehicle from it, the aim was to take a competition car and make it look like the humble hatchback. *(Author)*

CENTRE Doors were featherweight silhouettes of the original items, with only the most basic latches and fixed plastic windows – but plenty of stowage space. *(Author)*

RIGHT This was the view that rally crews wanted to see if they were setting off on an event in 1985–86. The sum of its parts made the Peugeot 205 Turbo 16 the most successful Group B car of all. *(Author)*

was outsourced to the specialist fabricator Heuliez. For 60 years this firm had been producing specialised coachwork such as station wagon conversions, many officially sanctioned by the manufacturer, and had also produced panels for the Citroën Visa Mille Pistes 'baby' Group B rally car as well as the mighty Renault 5 Turbo.

Final assembly of the 200 road cars and each batch of 20 example Evolution models for competition would take place at the old Simca factory in Poissy, where the monocoque, spaceframes, subframes and bodywork would all be brought together for the first time. Aerodynamically there was a minimum to worry about – and when the car was first unveiled in February 1983 it was completely bare of any wings or splitters, in

part because they were not yet designed and in part to retain the closest links possible to the all-important road car.

Even when the 205 Turbo 16 made its unofficial competition debut it had no aerodynamic appendages – although this would change shortly afterwards. Such was the unnerving habit of the car to throw its tail in the air that a modest rear wing was placed across the roof over what would, on a regular car, be the top of the hatchback.

When André de Cortanze produced the 205 Turbo 16 Evolution 2 in late 1984, a great deal had changed in the design and construction of the car. The most obvious change beneath the skin was that the two girder-like protrusions on either side of the engine bay had gone, replaced by a lighter, yet more rigid

BELOW The second evolution model of 1985–86 featured much less clutter and better access to the mechanical parts. Although it appears to be held together with fresh air, the structure was considerably stiffer. *(McKlein/ Slowly Sideways)*

ABOVE The Peugeot 205 Turbo 16 E2 is most easily distinguished by the aerodynamic enhancements – a fast whale tail rear wing on the roof trimmed out by twin canards on the front corners. *(Author)*

BELOW On both the evolutions of the rally car, fittings were retained wherever possible, such as the bonnet-mounted spotlights for the Safari Rally, intended to warn off wildlife and locals. *(McKlein/Slowly Sideways)*

spaceframe that made life much easier for the mechanics to reach in over.

All of the engine and rear-axle oil coolers were moved over to the left-hand side of the E2 engine bay to try and address the right-side bias in weight distribution, while the engine coolant radiator and air/water intercooler were relocated to the front of the car.

The front-to-rear weight balance was very close to 50/50 with the E2 version, but despite all of de Cortanze's best efforts there was still a distinct bias towards the right, courtesy of the offset engine layout. Minus fuel and the crew, the 205 Turbo 16 was 50kg heavier on the right-hand side, but by carefully juggling the fuel load beneath the front seats (and perhaps encouraging the co-driver towards a bit of weight loss) the bias could be pegged back to around 20kg.

Despite all of these measures to even up the mass within the car, moving in three dimensions is a very complicated business. As was shown every time that the Peugeots took off over a yump, the flight characteristics of the 205 Turbo 16 were unsettling to say the least.

The Peugeot 205 Turbo 16's flight path was severely affected by the gyroscopic effect of its transverse engine and gearbox through the rest of the transmission. The E2's wings had some effect but it was never cured. *(McKlein)*

Unquestionably it was this weakness that caused Ari Vatanen's catastrophic accident in Argentina, and which the engineers were never able to fully resolve, as witnessed by Shekha Mehtar's career-ending crash in the desert two years later (which also contributed to the death of Jacky Ickx's co-driver Christian Tarin on the 1991 Rallye des Pharaons).

The problem was gyroscopic rather than to do with weight distribution. Whenever the Peugeot 205 Turbo 16 (and its later derivatives) hit a bump and took off, the wheels, the driveshafts and the engine would all speed up and the effect of this would be to raise the car's nose. If the driver kept their foot on the gas this resulted in a tail-heavy landing at best, or at worst threatened to tip the car towards a backwards somersault.

But if the driver backed off dramatically, or touched the brakes, the gyroscopic effect would go dramatically the other way, throwing the tail higher into the air and precipitating a nosedive. Travelling at more than 100mph, and with a significant amount of weight behind the centre axis, landing on the nose would carry the tail up and over to send the car into an end-over-end roll of the kind that befell Vatanen, Mehta and Ickx.

To try and compensate for this nasty little surprise, de Cortanze fitted the biggest rear wing that he could to generate downforce that might help prevent the tail from rising – and increase the surface area to a point where, if the car did adopt a nose-down attitude, it might create enough air resistance to prevent it from going over.

The size of the wing was the subject of a long and voluble debate between Todt, de Cortanze and the FISA homologation team, and although it appears to be a vast whale tail, the Peugeot engineers always felt it should have been bigger. Peugeot's marketing team disagreed, however, and it is noticeable in

BELOW Timo Salonen shows off the full E2 aerodynamic package created by André de Cortanze as he presses on during the 1986 New Zealand event.
(McKlein/ Slowly Sideways)

LEFT **In search of greater downforce and unconstrained by FISA's regulations, Jean-Claude Vaucard hastily created a biplane rear wing using two standard units for the 1987 Pikes Peak hill climb.** *(McKlein)*

the official press shots of the E2 that it was photographed from angles and with lighting that did as much as possible to cover up the new structure.

To balance this new aerodynamic device, the team fitted canards on the front corners of the car to increase downforce on the front. The front and the rear wings both performed admirably at squashing the Peugeot down onto the road surface and cornering speeds leapt as a result. They did also provide some evening-out of the flight path but even so, the drivers were always wary about taking flight in a 205 Turbo 16.

In late 1986 it was clear that the Peugeots were coming to the end of their rally career – but new horizons beckoned them. Structurally, the cars changed comparatively little for the very different challenges presented by the Pikes Peak International Hill Climb and the Paris–Dakar Rally Raid.

The Pikes Peak cars were E2s taken from the existing stock in Peugeot Talbot Sport's workshops and treated to an extensive weight loss programme. Any of the trappings that came with having a co-driver in the car were removed, as were considerations such as the spare wheel and toolkit, the reserve fuel tanks and other ancillaries – anything at all that could reduce the mass of the cars.

Their coachwork was repainted for the trip, as by now Peugeot Talbot Sport had won a title sponsor in the form of RJ Reynolds tobacco and its big-spending Camel brand, which was taking the fight to Marlboro for the most visibility in motor sport. The distinctive, deep Camel yellow replaced white as the base colour on the livery, matching such other investments as the Lotus Formula 1 team and the Porsche 962s of privateer entrants Reinhold Joest and Walter Brun – although Jean Todt's signature stripes of blue, yellow and red remained firmly in place.

During testing, Ari Vatanen felt that the car was much too loose for his liking, with 650bhp available from its enlarged engine on the smooth gravel surface. For a driver who was still recovering from one major accident, the prospect of skittering along with a 1,500-metre drop over his shoulder was decidedly unappealing, and so the team on site, led by Jean-Claude Vaucard, fashioned a double-tier rear wing.

Thanks to a spot of back-of-a-fag-packet engineering, what the team produced was, quite literally, two of the standard roof-mounted whale tail spoilers stacked one upon the other with hastily fashioned endplates stuck on – together with a full-width rear wing to trim out the resulting downforce. For all its improvisation, the solution was to prove entirely

ABOVE When its world championship rally career was over, Jean Todt and his team went to conquer the Sahara with a car that bore relatively few changes – some more drastic than others. *(Peugeot)*

BELOW The additional 30cm centre section created a vast fuel tank for the many long stages on the 13,000km rally, while longer suspension travel with two springs and dampers per wheel were the major structural changes. *(McKlein)*

sufficient, and only a broken turbo pipe denied Vatanen victory at the very first attempt.

The cars that would race for 13,000km (8,080 miles) from Paris to Dakar were rather more substantially redesigned – but by less than might be imagined. The biggest single change was the insertion of an extra 30cm section in the middle of the car between the firewall and the engine. This cavernous 350-litre space became the location of the primary fuel tank – as did numerous other nooks and crannies (see Chapter 7).

The suspension was reconfigured to give the cars additional ground clearance, with longer, stouter wishbones that pushed the track an inch further out but gave a good six inches more stature. These were fitted with double coil-over dampers in preparation for crashing over Saharan sand dunes and numerous other hazards, both natural and man-made.

The engine and ancillaries needed to be beefed up to cope with the hostile environment, and to aid this process the air scoops on the 205's flanks were filled in and replaced with roof-mounted vents to feed the various water, oil and gearbox cooling processes. Beyond these changes, however, the cars would remain very much the same structurally as the 'Safari-spec' used in 1986 by their world championship-winning sisters.

Engine

A four-cylinder engine block cast from a single piece of alloy, with a specialist competition cylinder head boasting four valves per cylinder in 'v' formation was nothing new at Peugeot – it was exactly what the all-conquering Charlatans had built for the 1912 grand prix!

Seventy years of evolution in racing engines had apparently come full-circle.

The brand-new Peugeot XU family of engines was to feature heavily in the showroom Peugeot 205 series, so it was fitting that the unit was to provide the basis for the Turbo 16 for the marketeers as it was for the engineers. The turbocharged competition version, christened XU8T, used the more robust diesel block with removable cast iron wet cylinder liners sealed with O-rings.

ABOVE The 205 Turbo 16's deceptively rugged construction was tested to the utmost in Africa – but it bowed out unbeaten after conquering this majestic landscape. *(Peugeot)*

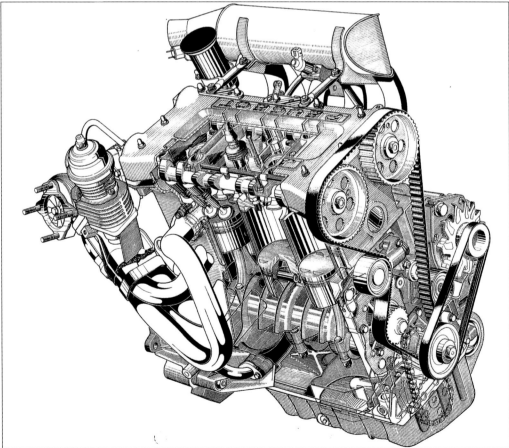

LEFT Taking what was to become the standard diesel engine block for the 205 road car and fitting it with a bespoke competition cylinder head created a genuine rallying powerhouse. *(Peugeot)*

In common with most competition engines it was run with a dry sump, with a constant supply of oil being pumped in from a tank on the firewall and feeding out via a heat exchanger to the catch tank. In common with the production models, the crankshaft was made from nitrided steel and sat on five lead/copper alloy bearings with forged steel connecting rods.

Aside from shortening the piston stroke to 82mm in order to bring the capacity down to 1,774.6cc, the most important element for the engineers was creating a new light alloy cylinder head with twin belt-driven overhead camshafts and four valves per cylinder. The valve heads were of 30mm diameter and made from nickel-chromium Nimonic alloy set on a 6.5mm diameter steel stem and controlled by helical springs within brass guides.

The engine of the first competition evolution cars was fed by a relatively straightforward Bosch K-Jetronic fuel injection system, in common with Audi's Group B Quattros and many other cars of the era. Also, like those cars, it did not take long for experiments to begin with greater electronic engine management to be brought into play, particularly as the available power from the turbo began to require ever-more precise management.

The turbocharger on all variants sat centrally within the chassis just behind the engine, while on the opposite side of the engine, up against the firewall, the inlet manifolds and fuel injection were housed. The original turbo was a KKK K26, another relatively standard off-the-shelf solution for competition cars including the Quattro and the Porsche 956 endurance racer, which was urging the engine up to a quoted 320bhp by the time of its world championship debut.

Another aspect of turbo performance, which the early XU8T had in common with similar engine setups, was excessive throttle lag leading in to eye-watering power delivery. This was no fun for drivers in lightweight Formula 1 cars or ground-effect sports cars, even with an

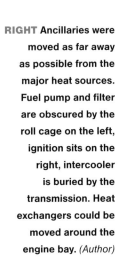

abundance of grip to help keep them on the windy side of care; for a rally driver pressing on at night on gravel or ice it could spell disaster.

The arrival of Jean-Pierre Boudy from the Renault Formula 1 team brought undoubtedly the greatest experience of turbocharging available within the motor sport industry. Boudy had devised the first turbocharged racing engines for Renault in endurance racing, Formula 1 and rallying, and developed a unique way of managing the dreaded turbo lag.

His system was known as DPV (*Dispositif Pre-rotation Variable*), which was essentially an early analogue form of the electronic anti-lag systems that would later became standard. DPV had been debuted by the Renault F1 team at the 1982 Monaco Grand Prix and was found to have given its drivers a huge increase in throttle response while turning the mad rush of power by providing a variable-section hole on the inlet side of the turbocharger which, in the E1, was linked mechanically to the throttle pedal.

At the first test of a DPV-equipped car, in the winter of 1983–84, both Jean-Pierre Nicolas and Ari Vatanen swore blind that the car went much slower with the DPV fitted. Having become accustomed to the rocket-from-a-bottle acceleration of the original turbo, they were convinced that Boudy had somehow watered down the effect of the turbo across the rev range.

A back-to-back test was conducted and, sure

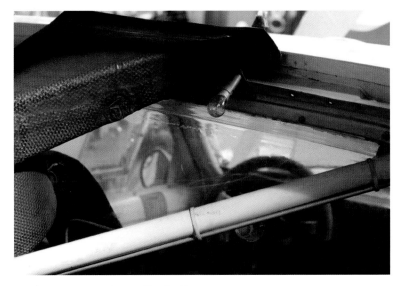

enough, the stage times of both drivers were roughly four-tenths of a second per kilometre faster with the DPV, and the car was considerably more driveable as a result. As ever, science brought home the bacon, and by early 1985 the team was able to run reliably with around 380–400bhp on tap, and the drivers were able to use the power band to the fullest.

The second evolution of the Peugeot 205 Turbo 16 saw considerable time and money invested in the engine, particularly the electronics (see below). The development of faster and more accurate engine management allowed for a steady increase in power, while vastly improving fuel efficiency and consumption.

ABOVE A small concession for the crews servicing at night was this light bulb mounted at the top of the firewall. *(Author)*

LEFT The full extent of ducting to feed the XU8T with fuel and air is routed throughout the vehicle and governed the amount of usable power that could be produced by Jean-Pierre Boudy's remarkable engine. *(Author)*

Neither the miles per gallon nor the emissions levels of the engines were of the remotest concern to anyone in the 1980s, but potentially running short of fuel on a long stage or road section were – and so too was the weight of fuel and its distribution within the overall mass of the car. And the opportunity to run more power was never turned away.

Fresh porting and manifold design on the second generation cylinder head, led by Boudy, enabled the E1's KKK turbocharger to be replaced by a much bigger Garrett T61. A minimum of 435bhp was available at 2.5 bar boost pressure, but 2.8 bar was possible, yielding around 500bhp. Irrespective of how much boost was being run, torque was improved in all areas of the rev band, reaching a practical optimum of 383lb ft when running 2.6 bar of pressure.

The original KKK turbo fed into an air/air intercooler but the limitations of such a design, particularly within the super-heated confines of the 205 T16 engine bay on events such as the Safari and Acropolis, brought about a rethink. The Garrett engine used an air/water intercooler that was electronically controlled and significantly more effective.

A heat exchanger for the water supply nestled within the impressive duct that was carved in above the left rear wheel arch, opposite that for the oil supply. Water would travel a considerable distance around the 205 Turbo 16, with the plumbing passing through to the nose-mounted radiator at the outer reaches of the circuit.

With all of the pipework in place, the engine bay of the 205 Turbo 16 became a very crowded place indeed. On the E2 version, André de Cortanze tried to unravel the cat's cradle somewhat, in order to afford his mechanics better access to where they needed to be as well as trying to solve the riddle of weight distribution. His enhancements included pushing the gearbox, engine and rear-axle oil coolers to the rear-left of the car, and throwing the engine coolant radiator and air/water intercooler to the front, which was a squeeze.

The E2 layout would remain basically unaltered from its debut on the 1985 Tour de Corse through to the end of the 205 Turbo 16's front-line career, on the Baja Aragōn in the summer of 1988. The only difference was that the post-World Rally Championship cars from 1987 onwards were no longer subject to the FIA's weights and measures department and the engineers could quite easily increase the engine capacity to 1,905cc with an adjustment

BELOW Peugeot would return to the WRC in 1998 with the 206 WRC, winning five more world championship titles in three years, using the same engine block as its illustrious forebear.
(McKlein)

to the stroke by 6mm, which became known as the XU9T.

Doing so opened up a new world in terms of available torque and power – although many of the figures bandied about regarding power outputs in the passage of nearly 40 years have been wide of the mark. The power of the engine was always tuned to the optimum level for each event, and unlike a drag race that could mean very different things at very different events.

The first evolution cars with KKK turbos started off with less than 340bhp and never knowingly went over 360bhp. The second generation Garrett cars with more sophisticated engine management could in theory run significantly more than that, but didn't often need to. On the Safari Rally, the cars were 'detuned' to 360bhp, while it was seldom run much beyond 475bhp on a five-day rally.

With the 1.9-litre XU9T engine there was a considerable upturn in available power and torque, both of which were put to good use. The real screamer among those engines was that which was used for the 11-minute blast up Pikes Peak in 1987, pushing out a little more than 650bhp. This is what became the base specification of the rallycross engines used in 1987–90 with championship-winning effect.

For the 13,000km trek across the Sahara to Dakar, torque was far and away the most treasured virtue, for pulling the cars up over mighty sand dunes or even the no less tricky obstacles laid out on the spectator stages in France. Pulling that torque further down the rev band to help the Peugeots dig themselves out of trouble was of primary importance, and such was the versatility of the engine's design that it was more than up to the job.

The XU engine would remain in PSA's front line well into the 21st century, and the architecture of the XU9T would be carried over into many of the group's later competition models – not the least of which being the Peugeot 206 WRC, its successor the Peugeot 307 WRC and the Citroën Xsara WRC which competed against it. In total, the 206 WRC brought home two drivers' world championships and three manufacturers' crowns, while the Xsara would claim three drivers' and three manufacturers' titles.

Transmission

Just like its engine, the gearbox of the Peugeot 205 Turbo 16 had its roots in PSA's showroom product line – albeit, in this instance, from a line that had long-since ended. It had first appeared within the glorious 1957 Citroën DS, but remained in service with its successor, the SM, until the late 1970s.

In the 1980s, the same unit was being put to very good use by sports car builders, including Maserati in the Merak and Lotus in the Esprit and Esprit Turbo – and it was also fitted in the C35 vans that Peugeot Talbot Sport used as service barges. The rationale for putting this redoubtable old unit in the Peugeot 205 Turbo 16 was very simple: cost.

The gearbox needed practically no modification to be repurposed, just a closing up of the ratios to make the car's progress through tortuous hairpins or across wet gravel as sharp as a new pin. The internal differential was disposed of in favour of a direct drive that plugged in to the Ferguson epicyclic unit that, by means of its viscous coupling, sent power to all four wheels by means of rigid shafts enclosed in a tube.

The Ferguson solution had the advantages of being lighter and cheaper than the Torsen centre differential preferred by Audi, and was the same basic design as that used by Lancia on the Delta S4, Austin Rover on the MG Metro 6R4 and Ford on the RS200 – only Citroën followed Audi down the Torsen route among the top class of Group B.

ABOVE Following on from Peugeot's turn-of-the-century success, between 2004 and 2012, sister brand Citroën won nine drivers' championships and eight manufacturers' championships, led by Sébastien Loeb. Six of those manufacturers' championships were won by the Xsara WRC (2003–05) and C4 WRC (2008–10), powered by turbocharged XU engines (the DS3 won in 2011–12, powered by a bespoke engine). *(McKlein)*

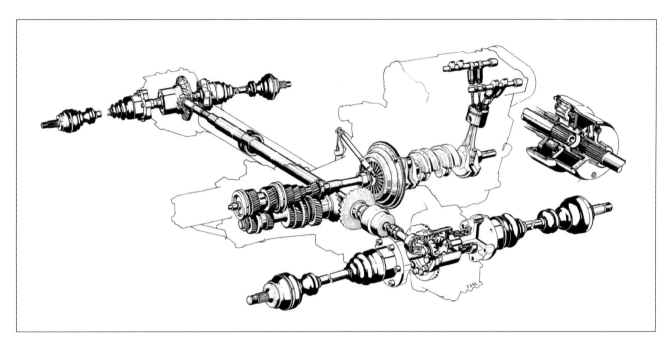

The division of power between front
and rear wheels could easily be adjusted
by changing the epicyclic gear ratio in the
Ferguson differential – a process that would
take eight minutes in total. On asphalt rallies it
was common to send 75% of the power to the
rear wheels and 25% to the front, with gravel
surfaces seeing 67% at the rear and 33% at
the front – which was the standard setting for
the 200 road cars when they went to
their owners.

The front and rear wheels were driven by
their own differentials, housed inside their own
cast magnesium casings and mounted within
the subframe. Each differential also had its

own limited slip settings, typically with 17% at
the front and 40% at the rear.

It was another of Des O'Dell's original
dicta that the final driveshafts to the hub
should all be of common size to minimise
cost and the workload required to change
them when out in the wilds – something for
which the mechanics would duly be grateful
for on many occasions.

Peugeot Talbot Sport deviated little from
its standard torque split settings for a long
time – the evidence of this being that, when it
did so at the 1986 Rally Argentina, there was
a disaster. The amount of torque sent to the
front wheels on that event was increased to

45%, with the result being that the magnesium housing burst open like a watermelon.

Stig Blomqvist drove at a measured pace in what was his debut for the team (and was already slightly unnerved by the car's behaviour after Vatanen's accident there a year earlier), and came home fourth. An aluminium casting was made for the front differential and hastily implemented for the 1000 Lakes a month later.

Beefing up transmission components was standard procedure for any rally team gaining experience – especially one whose potential power outputs climbed by 50% in the space of just over two years. The only other major alteration that the system needed was a six-speed derivative of the trusty PSA 'box, which was intended for use on the 1986 Safari, allowing closer ratios to be fitted in first-to-fifth with a longer gear in reserve for the long road sections involved. The six-speed did indeed become a regular feature of the setup, but not on the Safari, where it was a casualty of the ongoing spat between Jean Todt's office and that of the FIA president (see Chapter 6).

One advance that Peugeot Talbot Sport was working on that never saw the light of day was an electronically controlled centre differential to replace the 'spit-and-sawdust' Ferguson unit. As with all analogue four-wheel-drive cars, the 205 Turbo 16 was not at its best when turning into a corner, and in a combination of bends a driver

really had to be on top of their game to keep it pointing where they wanted it to go, through judicious use of the throttle and brake pedals.

With an onboard computer able to 'read' the inputs that were being made to the steering wheel, throttle and brake relative to the gear it was in, the differential could learn how to divide the power between the four wheels in the most helpful manner possible towards getting quickly through each corner.

Distilling these patterns into electronic algorithms was all the rage in the 1980s, with fuel injection, braking force and suspension travel all falling under the all-seeing eye of a little black box. While the Peugeot 205 Turbo 16 may not have been equipped with the last word in such systems, there was still some very clever data processing to be found on board.

Electronics

The first generation of Peugeot 205 Turbo 16 was born at almost the very moment, in 1983, when the Pandora's box of electronic wizardry was thrown wide open in the realm of motor sport.

Deep within the engineering Mecca that is Robert Bosch GmbH in Stuttgart, the use of computerisation to manage complex mechanical processes was something of a preoccupation. Bosch had long been a supplier to the German automotive and

ABOVE In 1992, Peugeot came close to taking this potential Ferrari-tamer to market: the Peugeot Oxia supercar. Its four-wheel-drive system was taken directly from the 205 Turbo 16.
(Getty Images)

ABOVE The little black box that governs every aspect of the Peugeot 205 Turbo 16's engine management requires kid gloves to handle. *(Author)*

ABOVE RIGHT The ignition was vital to the operation of engine management, allowing the computer to manage the relationship between the air speed and fuel delivery to optimum effect. *(Author)*

aerospace industries, through which a bulletproof relationship with Porsche reached back over decades.

In the early 1980s, the advent of turbocharging as a means to squeeze more performance from a car without increasing its engine size or fuel consumption was of significant interest. The OPEC oil crisis of 1973 was not easily forgotten, and the simplest way to evolve new technologies was to employ them in motor sport programmes.

At that time, across the majority of its major disciplines, FISA was attempting to create a very natural and orderly glass ceiling on the sport by setting a limit on fuel consumption. In endurance racing, a cap of 100 litres per hour was set at events over 1,000km and 108 litres per hour at the Le Mans 24 Hours. In Formula 1, a limit of 220 litres was imposed for each race.

At first, many teams sought to find more traditional routes around such obstacles to performance – the engineer's art that is commonly known as cheating. At the very simplest level, oversized fuel tanks could be disguised with such simple devices as an inflatable balloon in the bottom that could be inflated for inspection, when 220 litres would fill it to the brim, and deflated under racing conditions to give anything up to 20% more capacity.

There were other, darker secrets than that, but Porsche saw an opportunity to develop something relevant – and so too did Bosch. If the means of delivering the fuel to the cylinders could be made more intelligent, as it became through the ever-increasing computer power within the Motronic system, then the value

of every droplet within the fine mist pushed out by the fuel injectors grew exponentially – especially if the fuel itself was more potent.

In 1983–84, Peugeot adopted the customer electronic fuel injection system available from Bosch, called the K-Jetronic. Fundamentally, the quantity of fuel delivered to the cylinders was measured against the flow of air and continuously adjusted to ensure the optimum ratio for efficient combustion. The fuel pump provided the flow rate determined by the onboard computer, which also monitored inputs from the ignition to ensure that the whole system operated in unison from beginning to end.

The K-Jetronic was a workable system but it had some fairly severe limitations for competition use. Adding a turbocharger and adding to that Jean-Pierre Boudy's DPV system increased the complexities of the calculations that the system needed to consider exponentially, and without the same sort of partnership that Porsche enjoyed, it was unlikely that Bosch was going to provide an answer.

To compensate for the basic nature of its Bosch system, Peugeot first went to AET Thompson for assistance. Using a second set of inputs from the ignition, relating to the crankshaft's position and rotating speed and pressure within the air intake manifold, it was possible to complete a much more advanced hybrid that controlled the level of spark from the coil relative to the fuel flow.

This hybrid system worked well but with the Evolution 2 car for 1985–86 there would be more power, a different turbo and more complexity to be absorbed. Peugeot switched to a different, more comprehensive system with the second evolutionary model.

Fortunately, by that time just such a system was becoming available from Peugeot supplier and team partner Magneti Marelli. The Marelli-Solex engine management was specifically designed for complex competition engines such as the Ferrari 288 GTO, Lancia LC2 Group C car and the Lancia Delta S4 rally car. The Italian technology allowed Peugeot's engineers to further evolve the engine management with greater input from the turbocharger and wastegate, by electrically managing the DPV.

Rather than mechanically opening and closing the hole on the turbo inlet, the E2's system would calculate the appropriate hole size depending on throttle angle and charge gas temperature as it entered the cylinder head. This, linked in with the rest of the ignition and fuel injection data, is available today on even the humblest city car, but in 1985 this sat absolutely at the leading edge of the automotive electronics world.

Suspension and brakes

In many ways the running gear on which the Peugeot 205 Turbo 16 sat was its most conventional feature, but in others there was still room for a little innovation – primarily aimed at making maintenance easier on events.

LEFT The fuel pumps were controlled by the computer's ability to make calculations at breathtaking speed in order to summon up the ideal throttle response. *(Author)*

Identical subframes sat beneath the front and rear of the car, to which the upper and lower wishbones were mounted, each connecting to the hub. On each corner, single Bilstein coil-over dampers were fitted, the lower end of which connected to the top wishbone on the front suspension and directly onto the hub at the rear while their upper ends were bolted in to the sturdy mounts that had been fabricated into the car's structure.

Initial testing was conducted on asphalt, as would be expected of a French rally car, and test driver Jean-Pierre Nicolas felt the sort of cornering forces he had last experienced when racing at Le Mans. The downside of this race-

BELOW Resting on their identical front and rear subframes, the front and rear suspension units were anchored to the car on purpose-built turrets that were significantly further fore and aft of the standard car's. *(Peugeot)*

RIGHT Four-piston
calipers and 300mm
or 273mm ventilated
discs were standard fit
all round, depending on
the surface. *(McKlein)*

BELOW The right rear
corner had to bear the
most weight on the
205 Turbo 16 due to its
offset engine, causing
this to be a weak point.
On the E2 version
the co-driver could
douse it in water with
a foot-operated pump.
(McKlein)

ready setup became evident in the car's first outings on gravel, where it proved incredibly stiff and not only broke repeatedly but also made the car bounce around like a puppy.

Slowly but surely, the components were suitably reinforced and the optimum damping and spring rates were discovered, allowing the 205 to show its innate composure when cornering, even on the roughest surfaces such as the stages on the Acropolis Rally.

The main congenital weakness in the

suspension was that it would often fail under heavy load and in high temperatures on the right rear corner – the one that carried the largest load thanks to the offset of the engine. The friction within the right rear damper in particular would build up sufficient heat to bring about collapse and this was a shortfall that could only be put right with the second evolution of the breed.

Even after spreading the weight a little further throughout the car, there was little that André de Cortanze could do about the mass of the engine. The E2 version nevertheless had temperature sensors on the right rear shock absorber which would trigger a light on the dashboard in front of the co-driver, who in turn had a foot-operated pedal that was connected to an electric water pump.

When the light came on, the co-driver could trigger the pump and cold water would be liberally sprayed over the errant damper until it was back within its safe operating temperatures. This was a regular fixture of life for the co-driver in an E2 on most surfaces because the stiffness in the suspension had to be increased by 50% in order to cope with the increased load from the aerodynamic wings and the sharply increased forces of acceleration and deceleration that came with the car's upgraded performance.

Deceleration was provided by ventilated disc brakes all round. On the road car and on the first competition cars, the front calipers were taken from the Citroën BX while the rears were also to be found on the Renault Fuego, activated by two independent circuits and supported by an imposing 9in (23cm) diameter servo.

Steering, wheels and tyres

The steering mechanism of the Peugeot 205 Turbo 16 was a simple, robust rack-and-pinion design that required two-and-a-half turns to go from one lock to the other, and it would remain in place throughout the vehicle's active life. In its initial form it was extremely basic, however, with no power assistance to help the drivers.

With the arrival of Timo Salonen in 1985, the chain-smoking Finn soon felt considerable discomfort while driving. He was renowned for taking most corners with only one hand on the wheel and to aid him an inlet camshaft-driven hydraulic power steering system was introduced at the Sanremo Rally, which Salonen duly won.

Throughout its life, the wheels and tyres for the Peugeot 205 Turbo 16 came from two partners to the team: Speedline and Michelin. Speedline created the robust and versatile wheel known as the 'pepperpot' specifically for the programme, and then later when the Peugeot 205 GTI 'hot hatchback' went on sale a more domestically suited version of its rally wheel was fitted as standard, giving the 1.6-litre car its iconic looks.

Overheating brakes were an issue for all teams on the Tour de Corse, one that could also affect cars entered by Peugeot importers on some asphalt rounds of their national series. Initially, Speedline created a finned disc that would fit within the hub and draw heat out and away from the brakes, but this was replaced in 1986 with a bespoke design that was lighter and significantly more efficient at clearing out hot air.

The final variant of wheel made available to Peugeot Talbot Sport was the eight-spoke design that could cope with asphalt and smooth gravel surfaces, which was used in Sanremo and the Pikes Peak hill climb. In all cases, the wheels were mated to Michelin TRX tyres and, once the hurdle of Speedline's imperial 15-inch wheels and Michelin's uncompromising metrification was overcome, they provided exactly the support that Jean Todt demanded.

ABOVE Fifteen-inch Speedline 'pepperpot' cast magnesium wheels were standard for the 205 Turbo 16 throughout its life. Here the lightweight 8-inch version on the left wears a wet weather road tyre while the narrower reinforced 7-inch at the rear wears a full gravel tyre. *(Author)*

BELOW Three other wheel designs appeared on the 205 Turbo 16, all of which were primarily to ease cooling on asphalt events. In 1985 finned rotors were added as a temporary measure to help cool the brakes before bespoke designs followed in 1986. *(McKlein)*

Fuel and lubricants

By the time that the Peugeot 205 Turbo 16 was in development, turbocharging had been a major force in motor sport for more than a decade. It was Porsche that first popularised the turbo in 1972 when its mighty Le Mans-winning 917 went to America for Can-Am racing, and the team bolted a turbo to its flat-12 engine in order to compete with home-grown Detroit muscle.

In its first season, with a modest 750bhp on tap, Porsche won the Can-Am title at its first attempt. Then the team went all-out in 1973 and produced a 5.4-litre engine with a bigger turbo that could turn out up to 1,580bhp. A much milder Porsche turbo engine was meanwhile debuted in a modified 911 at Le Mans that same year, leading to the development of a rash of turbo-powered sports prototypes and GTs appearing at the Circuit de la Sarthe in 1976 – the turbo era was underway.

A major factor in the success of Porsche's turbo development throughout the late 1960s and early 1970s was its fuel and lubricant partner, Shell. The Anglo-Dutch firm had, through its technical centres in Germany and Britain, already gained long experience of working with prodigiously powerful engines

and forced induction which dated as far back as the Mercedes-Benz and Auto Union grand prix teams of the 1930s.

Fuel composition later became a major factor in the air war of 1939–45, and in Germany the development of 'super-fuels' was something of a preoccupation, based upon experience from the grand prix engines. These 'super-fuels' required the use of aromatic petrochemicals such as benzene, toluene and xylene.

In the 1980s, the regulation of fuels was an inexact science that only demanded that they be similar to that used in road cars with a maximum octane rating of 102 and, in 1982–83, when BMW was attempting to make its turbocharged Formula 1 engine competitive, it decided to go back into the archives.

BMW's engineers dusted off the fuel formulae used in the company's turbocharged engines built for high-altitude Focke-Wulf Fw190 fighters during the war (a blend not dissimilar to that used by the pre-war grand prix teams). By using toluene as a base for the fuel, it would ignite more slowly than standard gasoline, making it better suited to the highly charged confines of a turbo engine, while also producing significantly more energy when it did combust – leading to the dramatic

RIGHT Shell was the most experienced fuel and lubricants company working with turbocharged engines, and had powered Porsche to success at Le Mans and in Formula 1.
(Getty Images)

escalation in power output seen in all forms of motor sport during the 1980s.

By juggling the compounds in each blend, scientists at all of the fuel companies were able to optimise the performance of their product while keeping within the magic 102 octane limits set down by the governing body. Although they met the regulations of the sport as 'standard fuel', the presence of high levels of aromatics became immediately obvious, due to the distinctive scent that gives them their name. That is why standing next to a turbocharged Group B rally car in period was often an eye-watering experience, thanks to aromatic-enriched exhaust fumes.

Aromatics are used to this day for a variety of industrial processes and the production of consumer goods such as clothing, packaging, paints, adhesives, plywood, computer casings, compact discs, dyes, agrochemicals, pharmaceuticals and many more among them. They are, however, universally banned from fuel composition because, even in low doses, exposure can lead to tiredness, confusion, weakness, nausea, and affect sight and hearing. Higher doses, even just for a short period, can lead to unconsciousness or death.

Drivers in the Group B era would often complain of suffering from an overdose of fumes from the fuel, such as Juha Kankkunen on the 1986 RAC Rally. In the mid-engined, turbocharged cars the only place to put the fuel tanks was beneath the seats, and there is a school of thought that suggests that Henri Toivonen may have been affected by fumes prior to the crash that killed him and co-driver Sergio Cresto.

In the motor sport world of the 1980s, nobody worried unduly about these sorts of details. To team members, the greater hazard was standing in any spilt fuel, which would quickly melt the soles of your boots. It also meant that fuel lines and seals needed to be made from more durable materials than the standard rubbers and plastics in order to prevent the fuel from dissolving them.

In the early 1980s, Shell's long-standing technical and commercial partnership with Porsche ensured that its products were in the title-winning Porsche 956 in endurance racing and the McLaren Formula 1 team with TAG-Porsche engines. It made perfect sense for Peugeot to pursue a similar arrangement, with Shell proudly taking the most visible areas of the car as sponsor, in order for Peugeot Talbot Sport to reap the rewards of a combined turbo fuel programme that was the biggest of its kind at the time.

BELOW Every turbocharged racing engine ran with a mix of up to 86% toluene in the mid-1980s as engineering and science combined to draw the maximum energy from the minimum quantity of fuel. *(McKlein)*

Chapter Five

The team's view

The history of the Peugeot 205 Turbo 16 reveals a cast of characters who would shape Peugeot Talbot Sport, its most celebrated creation and the sport of rallying as it existed in the Group B era. Their successes and failures were of a magnitude beyond anything seen before or since: the time when rallying was the greatest show on Earth.

OPPOSITE The Peugeot 205 Turbo 16 became the first and only purpose-built rally car to triumph at the top level of international rallying, thanks in no small part to the men and women who created it. *(McKlein)*

The ringmaster

German engineers may have invented the motor car but the French invented motor sport and they have been ever-present in administering its passage throughout almost 140 years. As a result, the governing body of the sport is called the Fédération Internationale de l'Automobile (FIA), and its offices sit squarely on the Place de la Concorde, at the opposite end of the Avenue Champs-Élysées to the Arc de Triomphe in Paris's celebrated 8th arrondissement.

Jean-Marie Balestre's rise to the head of this organisation is fascinating in itself. Born in 1921, he would often claim to have fought against Franco in the Spanish Civil War – although he would still have been of school age at the time. In fact, very little evidence supports any of the colourful claims that Balestre made about his youth, from where he studied to his early outings as a sports journalist.

Balestre proudly told of having been in the French army when Germany invaded in 1940, but later research uncovered that he was in jail for fraud offences at the time and was only released after the shooting was over. Upon his release, Balestre made his way to Paris where he would ultimately join forces with pro-Nazi agitator Robert Hersant, who founded the magazine *Jeune Force* to appeal to French youth and promote the denunciation of Jewry and support of Hitler.

In 1943, Balestre joined the SS. Various photographs and documents were preserved after the war's end, some of which were made public 30 years later, as he was ascending through the senior levels of the FIA. Balestre claimed that it was a cover under which he was able to support the Resistance with inside information and that the Germans had uncovered his duplicity and sent him to Dachau just as the war ended. If anyone dared to question his version of events they usually ended up in court, where the judges tended to find in Balestre's favour because there was no evidence that contradicted his story – although he was only ever awarded notional damages.

In fact, Balestre probably did spend time in the notorious concentration camp – albeit when it was under American occupation and a good number of former SS members were interned there. In the end he returned to Paris and was reunited with Robert Hersant, working for his old boss as he established a new media group that ultimately included the daily newspaper *Le Figaro* and the motoring magazine *Auto Journal*. This latter title allowed Balestre to immerse himself in the world of motor sport, in particular in encouraging young French racers. To this end he became a major player in the emerging world of karting and, by the early 1970s, Balestre was made president of the FIA's international karting committee, the CIK.

From here, Balestre worked to create a new branch office of the FIA that was solely occupied with the business of motor sport, the Fédération Internationale de Sport Automobile (FISA), which relieved the FIA of the burden of catering to the racing community directly. Balestre excelled in the role and then, when the presidency of the FIA itself came up for grabs, he threw his hat in the ring. It was at this time that the photographs emerged of Balestre in his SS uniform, but they did little to sway the voting and he was duly elected as president of the FIA in 1978.

From the president's office, Balestre approached motor sport with the eye of a journalist and the theatricality of P.T. Barnum; seeking only to tell the biggest possible stories and create the biggest possible headlines, not

RIGHT As president of the FIA, Jean-Marie Balestre created a new world order for motor sport in the 1980s of which Group B was an integral part to bringing new interest to the sport. *(McKlein)*

only in Formula 1 but also across the gamut of sports cars, touring cars and rallying. With this mindset, Balestre sought to simplify many of the arcane rules and regulations that governed his pre-eminent sporting categories, paving the way towards Group A for volume production cars, Group B for high-performance sports cars and specialist vehicles and finally Group C for prototype cars.

Within these basic groups the rules and regulations were tweaked to encourage the most spectacular engineering possible and the most entertaining battles between manufacturers – who duly thronged to take part in almost every discipline of the sport, aided by an abundance of commercial sponsorship from tobacco, alcohol, technology and lifestyle brands.

On Balestre's watch, Formula 1 was revived from being a minority sport populated with homemade Cosworth-powered specials to a global automotive powerhouse. Endurance racing and the Le Mans 24 Hours gloried in Group C regulations that brought in glamour and money on an unprecedented scale. Group A saloon cars entertained fans in domestic and international battles. But the real genie that was released from the bottle was Group B.

The economics of motor sport dictate that it is invariably more expensive to turn a car designed for getting from A to B into a top-class competition machine than it is to start from scratch. Through the 1970s, the likes of Ford and Fiat lavished astronomical sums on taking three-box saloon cars off the production line and turning them into Porsche-beaters. Seeing cars like the Ferrari 308 scrabbling

ABOVE LEFT Group A became the FIA's premier 'showroom' class for touring car racing and rallying, drawing colossal interest from teams and manufacturers. *(McKlein)*

ABOVE Limited only by fuel consumption, Group C sports prototypes delivered unprecedented spectacle, thanks largely to the ready supply of competitive Porsche 956s (and later 962s) for private teams. *(McKlein)*

to keep up with a Ford Escort confused the public and embarrassed the prestige brands, so encouraging all of the cars to be built as exotic competition specials would, in theory, level the playing field and potentially save cost.

Most of the manufacturers intending to participate in Group B had already committed

BELOW The Renault 5 Turbo was a wild mid-engined derivative of a humble French hatchback that helped forge the FIA's vision for Group B. *(Author)*

Although it is often claimed in motoring histories that the man who was ultimately responsible within Peugeot for the 205 Turbo 16 was the son of Peugeot's fabled grand prix ace Georges Boillot, facts have a rather unfortunate way of dispelling this myth. Georges Boillot was shot down and killed in the skies over Verdun in 1916, while Jean Boillot was not born until 1926.

Neither was he the offspring of Georges' younger brother André Boillot, a notable racer for Peugeot under the pseudonym Dribus in the days after World War One. André died after crashing a Peugeot 201 during practice for the 1932 Ars hill climb but, while the timing was better suited to the mythology, in truth Boillot is simply a very common family name in the Doubs region of France. Jean Boillot's father was a hotelier called Arthur.

After studying law and business management at a university in Paris, Jean Boillot's first employer was the bank Crédit Lyonnais, where he rapidly rose through the ranks of young managers before returning home to the Doubs region at the age of 28 to join Peugeot.

His career trajectory continued and by the age of 35 he was handed the senior management role of Peugeot's Canadian importer, returning to France six years later with a wife and three children. By 1976 he was a member of the controlling board at the head of the company, and in 1982 he was named CEO of the by-now troubled group as it prepared to launch the new Peugeot 205, itself a project in which Boillot had played a key role from the outset.

Dominique de Guibert was head of Peugeot product testing at the time and regularly received visits from Boillot at the company's development facilities at its Sochaux plant. 'Each month, he came to spend an afternoon at Belchamps on the test track of Peugeot', said de Guibert. 'I made him try cars. When he climbed in, he touched the materials and when he drove he loved the speed and he listened to the car.'

In the midst of such corporate anxiety over the success of the 205, the travails of Peugeot

BELOW Jean Boillot (left) stands with Jean Todt and Ari Vatanen in Monaco, celebrating their historic victory at the start of the 1985 season. *(Getty Images)*

Talbot in motor sport must have seemed like a welcome relief with which to concern himself. As a board member, Boillot knew the fine details and financial commitments that it was making in order to support the Talbot sponsorship of Guy Ligier's Formula 1 team (and to servicing its engines), as well as the costs of the works Peugeot rally team and Des O'Dell's Talbot operation in the UK.

There can be little doubt that it was clear to someone with even a fraction of Boillot's acumen that PSA was encumbered with too many brands competing against one another, at great cost, for the same customers.

Today such brand differentiation within one manufacturing group is considered highly desirable as it allows the parent company to push out volume products while subsidiaries offer the feeling of more bespoke products – all of which are mechanically identical, such as the Volkswagen Polo, Audi A1 and Škoda Fabia. Before such badge engineering was the norm, however, a healthy dose of streamlining was going to be required and the axe would always fall fastest upon the former Chrysler brands, so easing back the throttle on Talbot's motor sport programmes and their publicity was an expedient move.

In contrast to Talbot, Peugeot had never really been a top-flight motor sport organisation. It was simply a tiny microcosm of life at the Sochaux factory – albeit a proud one, with a history of strong results from African rallies to its credit. It was not the sort of organisation upon which to pin the marketing programme of the 205, however, and so Boillot was delighted to find a saviour in the form of Jean Todt, who brought undeniable expertise and knowledge of the sport together with a clear-eyed and ruthlessly corporate approach to its management.

Todt may have been the hatchet man who killed off the previous generation of competition departments within PSA, but there was no doubt as to whose authorisation he carried: that of Jean Boillot.

to their first-generation cars by the time that the Audi Quattro arrived. As a result, the cars that debuted through 1982 and 1983 were relatively modest rear-wheel-drive cars based largely on their Group 4 predecessors, albeit considerably lightened and with their power increased.

Opel, Toyota and Nissan began competing with these modest Group B machines but Ford's Escort RS1700T was cancelled once the Audi Quattro's potential was revealed. Renault's hyperactive little 5 Turbo was still competitive on asphalt but Lancia, stepping back into the ring after Fiat's successful tenure in the world championship, went an altogether different route.

The 037 was Group B in its purest form, exactly as Jean-Marie Balestre had envisioned it. It was a modern, turbocharged Stratos: a bantamweight chassis with a mid-mounted supercharged engine, sinfully beautiful bodywork and capable of taking on the Audi Quattro on all but the roughest events. The 037 also reaffirmed that putting the engine

TOP Opel's Manta 400 was typical of early Group B machinery, being a lightened and more powerful iteration of its Group 4 Ascona. *(Author)*

ABOVE The Lancia 037 Rallye first appeared in mid-1982 and was the archetypal Group B car envisioned when the rules were created. It claimed the 1983 manufacturers' title, but rear-wheel-drive had little chance of keeping pace with four-wheel-drive much longer. *(McKlein/Slowly Sideways)*

behind the crew was the ideal solution in the eyes of everyone at Peugeot Talbot Sport but, to give the team its best possible chance of success, they would have to build it with four-wheel-drive. Fortunately, the team had all of the backing it needed to develop such a car.

Flashpoint – the FIA vs. the manufacturers

In 1984, the motor sport world was still emerging from beneath the mushroom cloud that marked where Jean-Marie Balestre's FISA, the global legislative body, ran headlong into Bernie Ecclestone's FOCA, the Formula One Constructors' Association, representing the collective commercial interests of the British-based grand prix teams.

For more than two years, FISA and FOCA had battled over perceived bias in the sport's officials and for the sporting and commercial future of Formula 1. Ecclestone wanted the power to negotiate TV contracts and trackside sponsorship deals, merchandising and hospitality, in order to share the bounty between the teams and the event promoters (with a healthy margin for himself). Balestre was incensed by the assertions.

The end result was the Concorde Agreement, under which all of the teams agreed to appear at every world championship event, rather than picking and choosing those that suited their budgets if the revenues from the races were distributed more evenly between them. So began a period of entente cordiale that was shattered in 1984 when

Ecclestone convinced the Automobile Club de Monaco to agree a big bucks TV deal with ABC for its international events.

In response to what he saw as an incursion on his presidency, Balestre took the ACM to task for selling FISA's events: cancelling the 1985 Monaco Grand Prix and threatening to remove the club's status as a sanctioning body, endangering the Monte Carlo Rally. For the ACM president Michel Boeri, a long-time supporter of Balestre, this was too draconian and he began legal proceedings, which served only to entrench the FIA president's position further.

For the motor manufacturers who had invested so much in Group B rallying as a showcase, this threat to the marquee event of their season was unacceptable – and to none more so than Peugeot. Jean Todt and Jean Boillot could settle for nothing less than victory in Monte Carlo for the 205 Turbo 16, and led the manufacturers to seek recourse through the BPICA (the Bureau Permanent International des Constructeurs d'Automobiles).

This set the global authority for motor manufacturing on a collision course with the global authority for motoring organisations. The Monte Carlo Rally was removed from the points-scoring rounds of the World Rally Championship.

The BPICA escalated the conflict to parliamentary level, successfully lobbying the French government on a matter of key importance to Renault and Peugeot as competitors in the series as a major element of their global sales strategy. Members of François Mitterand's government teamed up with Prince Rainier's officials to try to force Balestre to back down.

Ultimately the ACM's legal challenge failed, but with the muscle of the BPICA behind him, Michel Boeri was still able to negotiate a settlement in which the club handed its lucrative TV deal over to Balestre in return for a negotiated annual payment. Both sides claimed victory but Balestre was harbouring dark thoughts. He could do little about Bernie Ecclestone, who was ultimately the author of the drama, but at least he had a target for his ill humour: the manufacturers.

The moment at which Balestre first chose to rattle his sabre was immediately after the 1985 1000 Lakes – speaking in acid terms about

BELOW Bernie Ecclestone and Jean-Marie Balestre had called a truce in the FISA–FOCA war for control of Formula 1, but Ecclestone was quite happy to encourage the Monegasque authorities to act on his behalf. *(Motorsport Images)*

certain French manufacturers just as Jean Todt and Peugeot Talbot Sport were celebrating their first drivers' and manufacturers' championship titles. It must, therefore, have been a doubly satisfying moment for Jean Todt to have received the Légion d'l lonneur for his services to French motor sport – an honour that Balestre's wartime past precluded him from receiving. To compound the FIA president's ill humour, the BPICA voted the 1985 Monte Carlo Rally as the best motoring event of the year.

LEFT Michel Boeri, president of the Automobile Club de Monaco, triggered the first crisis of the Group B era as the FIA threatened to remove the Monte Carlo Rally from the 1985 world championship, prompting the manufacturers to act. *(Motorsport Images)*

GROUP S: THE EVOLUTION OF THE BREED

FISA had originally announced that Group B regulations would come into force from 1 January 1982 and provide stability for a minimum of five years – namely until 1 January 1987. In the event, the vast majority of manufacturers weren't ready with their Group B cars at the start of the 1982 season, and as a result Group B only began to be used as a designation for the top class at that year's Rally Brazil on 11–14 August.

By 1985, it was clear that the Peugeot 205 Turbo 16 had changed everything. Here was a manufacturer prepared to spend whatever it took in order to make a lightweight spaceframe mid-engined car with the additional benefits of four-wheel-drive. It was eventually followed by the MG Metro 6R4, Lancia Delta S4 and Ford RS200.

Nobody was more surprised than FISA by the scale of manufacturer investment that Group B attracted, and therefore by the mind-blowing performance that the cars offered. With power output soaring and the convoys of service vehicles including fuel bowsers laden with toluene-rich 'rocket fuel', something had to be done. Remarkably, what happened next met with almost universal approval.

In mid-1985, FISA stated that Group B would be given a stay of execution until 1 January 1988, fulfilling its pledge of rules stability for five years and giving the manufacturers another 12 months of wiggle room. That wiggle room would be needed to prepare for an evolution of the current rules: Group S.

Group S would be an engine formula that limited the manufacturers to 300bhp through either a 1.2-litre turbo engine or a 2.4-litre naturally aspirated unit. Everything else about the car would be free in terms of construction, transmission, aerodynamics and suspension but rather than produce 200 road-going cars and then 20 examples of each competitive 'evolution', they need only build 10 cars in total to gain homologation.

To most of the cost-conscious manufacturers this meant that they could simply repurpose their existing Group B cars with the new smaller engines but greater technical freedom. Undoubtedly they would explore new avenues in terms of transmission and aerodynamics but they were still going to save money hand-over-fist by being able to carry over their current kit.

Then came 1986, when the sum of all fears about Group B was realised.

ABOVE Peugeot never commenced work on a running prototype Group S car, but did display this mock-up of the Peugeot 405 that would have formed its basis at the 1986 Paris Motor Show. In modified form, this design would win the 1988 Pikes Peak hill climb and become the primary Rally Raid car in the later years of the programme. *(Peugeot)*

Living with Jean Todt

To many motor sport enthusiasts, Jean Todt is something of a cold and distant figure: aloof from the passions that his decisions and his teams have stirred throughout his long years at Peugeot, Ferrari and later as president of the FIA. Yet within the teams that he presided over there is a sense of unshakeable confidence and eagerness to please a boss who would stop at nothing to ensure that his engineers, drivers, strategists and staff had the best possible preparations for success.

'Nissan had never thought [of winning] any world championship titles; they just participated in the rallies that could be beneficial in the marketing', reflected Seppo Harjanne, co-driver for Timo Salonen. 'That was the criteria for how they picked the rallies. We did not do any full seasons. I think if the whole season was ten rallies, we did eight or nine at most... We never aimed fully for the world title. At Peugeot that was then our sole goal.'

The drivers and co-drivers formed a very small percentage of the team overall. At full strength for an event, Peugeot Talbot Sport mustered three Peugeot 504 support cars, three Peugeot 205 Turbo 16 recce cars and a road-going Turbo 16 chase car that was put at Jean Todt's disposal. Four large trucks were held with the majority of spare parts, while three Peugeot C35 vans acted as the service barges, supported by a Shell fuel bowser, two Aerospatiale Squirrel helicopters and one fixed-wing aircraft. Total event personnel was 60 – 33 on the ground and 27 travelling by air, including a doctor, a masseur and even a cordon bleu chef.

Todt's team was operating at another level entirely to the rest of the World Rally Championship operations – even the much-vaunted Audi Sport. If anything, Audi's ability to squander the advantage that its turbocharged four-wheel-drive Quattros had enjoyed was an inspiration to Todt in how not to approach team management. In Todt's view, Audi should have swept to both the drivers' and manufacturers' titles in 1981, 1982, 1983 and 1984, but they had won only 50% of those available before the Peugeot Talbot Sport team hit its stride – an unacceptable level of performance, in Todt's estimation.

Growing up in the suburbs of Paris during the 1950s, the short, slight and outwardly placid figure of Jean Todt was consumed with a burning ambition to become involved in motor sport. His father was a Jewish refugee from Poland who had lost almost his entire family during the war, and he urged his son towards caution and the need to get a good education.

Rather than poring over his schoolbooks, the young Todt joined the youth wing of AGACI, the association of independent racing teams. His academic career shambled along in comparison with the youngster's networking among the Parisian motor sport community, and in 1964 the 18-year-old convinced his father to trade in the family's Renault Dauphine for a Mini-Cooper.

With this car, Todt went off one weekend, telling his parents that he was going to stay at a friend's. In fact, he handed the keys over to another keen young member of the AGACI whom Todt believed had the right stuff to be a driver, while he himself sat alongside to guide him.

Typically for Todt, he told his parents immediately about the deception before they heard about it any other way. Rather than censure the boy, the elder Todt swapped his Mini for a Triumph TR4, which also spent its weekends in competition.

Finally, in 1969, 23-year-old Jean Todt made his professional debut as a co-driver with the factory NSU team. The more appearances he made, the more connections he grew and for the next ten years he was to be found guiding Finns, Frenchmen, Swedes and Englishmen through rallies around the world in a vast array of machines – and usually with success.

By 1980, Todt was the regular co-driver for the poster boy of French rallying, Guy Fréquelin. Together they joined Talbot, where a number of senior figures including Corrado Provera and Olivier Quesnel lobbied for Todt's cool, analytical mind to be brought to bear upon PSA Group's motor sport department, leading to the Peugeot 205 Turbo 16.

When the car was first revealed to the world, in February 1983, Todt was very quick to highlight the collective effort that had gone into this new French supercar. 'We didn't copy the others, we had a little delay to take advantage

of', he said. 'I wish to insist on [paying tribute] because our engineers have achieved a real feat of making a car from A to Z in 14 months precisely... we are the pioneers with a transverse central rear engine car and four-wheel-drive.'

As far as Todt was concerned, the team's mission was clear: Peugeot had taken the leap of faith to spend extravagant sums of money to leverage success in rallying as a tool to sell cars and save the company. The car was the star and Peugeot was the story – which is why he did not break the bank to sign drivers like Markku Alén or Walter Röhrl. He approached them, offering the best car, but if their demands were too great he walked away and found drivers who were good enough to do the job without stealing all the limelight.

The first driver whom Todt selected to lead the team was Ari Vatanen, whose win-or-crash approach to the sport seemed completely at odds with the Frenchman's methodology. Yet if Vatanen seemed an odd choice for Todt, those who knew the Finn also believed that Peugeot was not a natural fit for him either.

'It was a jump into an unknown in a way', Vatanen recalled, 'because there was one particular British mechanic who advised me definitely not to go. Because he had been working with Talbot and he had been with the French and he said: "no it will never work with this middle-engined car and you know what the French are like – they will only use French suppliers and French distributors and fit French tyres and it's a French workplace and you mustn't go there."

'Anyway, there were a lot of doubts at that time, how would a mid-engine four-wheel-drive car work? Really people were positive that concept will not work but I had a good feeling right from the beginning when I spoke to Jean Todt and I saw the mechanics and I saw Jean-Claude Vaucard and I just felt – these are the things you can't measure, you just feel. You look into their eyes and you realise that something will come out of this.'

Something did come out of this – five successive rally victories between late 1984 and early 1985. Nevertheless, Vatanen had

fallen short in Todt's opinion, whether by crashing, as he had in Corsica and on the RAC Rally (even if he was able to recover and win), or by pushing the car to breaking point, as he had on the Acropolis. A fast but steady hand was needed at the wheel of the second car for 1985 to maximise manufacturer points.

'After the 1000 Lakes Rally he called and asked if it would be possible for me to drive one of their cars', said Timo Salonen. 'And for me it was wonderful news to be asked to come and work with them.'

For Salonen and his co-driver Seppo Harjanne, the world that Todt had created for his team in Paris was far removed from that of other rally teams such as Nissan. Everything was bigger, brighter and more opulent – including the travel arrangements.

'Initially we flew in economy because we were two stingy guys!' said Harjanne. 'Before, we got everything from Nissan in one bunch of notes and with that money we had to pay all the flights, allowances, everything... In the beginning [at Peugeot] we wanted to save money but pretty soon learnt the household rules.'

For Juha Kankkunen, the difference between Peugeot Talbot Sport and his old team at Toyota was equally marked. Despite the scale of Jean Todt's operation in Paris, however, his attention to detail was clear from the outset.

'When he came to the factory every morning he would shake everybody by the hand', Kankkunen remembered. 'Everybody, you know: "Good morning boys, how are you, thanks for doing this or that". Very diplomatic. Good person to handle the things for the team. He also was basically the guy who lifted Peugeot up from bankrupt, you know, and he managed all the things that needed to be done – he did a good job. A lot of politics as well, and he was good at that, but he was just the boss.'

Kankkunen's description of Jean Todt hits the nail on the head. Unlike several of his most respected contemporaries in rallying, like Ove Andersson at Toyota or Roland Gumpert at Audi, Todt had no real mechanical knowledge. He was an organiser and administrator, a deft politician and a leader, who no doubt would describe his role in the same way as Enzo Ferrari once described his own: an 'agitator of men'.

'Like he says himself, he protects his privacy and is not tapping the backs of everybody and having a round of beers – that's not his style at all', Ari Vatanen recalled. 'But he has always very well looked after his drivers and it's not that he would say "if you don't drive well you will not drive again" because the worst thing to do is provide more pressure on a driver. I remember in '85 he said: "Well, you know Ari, the first half of the season hasn't gone so well but I know you can do better so let's make the

contract now already for next year." That was his approach: "You have the contract but if the second half of the season is not good, well, maybe you can't drive for me anymore." So you say to him "Wow – so you trust me?" And then of course the second half of the season will go well.'

The bitter end – and beyond

The denouement of Group B rallying was a series of bitter blows that sparked still greater hostility between Jean-Marie Balestre's FIA and the competing manufacturers, particularly Peugeot. Before then, however, the year began with the scintillating prospect of Jean Todt's team at the top of its game taking

ABOVE A place for everything and everything in its place. Peugeot Talbot Sport wanted for nothing under Jean Todt's stewardship. *(McKlein)*

BELOW Precisely drilled and with the confidence of their 1985 season behind them, Peugeot Talbot Sport went into 1986 as the team to beat. *(McKlein)*

on the wealth of new mid-engined four-wheel-drive challengers to its crown.

Honours were even between the two leading teams, Peugeot and Lancia, when the field arrived in Portugal. Lancia had won in Monte Carlo and Peugeot had won in Sweden, but the new Fords looked threatening, based upon the pace that they had shown on their debut.

After the first three asphalt stages in Portugal, Lancia held first, second and third places with two seconds covering Miki Biasion, Markku Alén and Henri Toivonen. The Peugeots of Kankkunen and Salonen, the MG Metro 6R4s of Malcolm Wilson and Tony Pond plus the lone Audi Sport Quattro S1 of Walter Röhrl were locked in their own battle a few seconds behind.

By then, however, it had been confirmed that there had been terrible carnage on the opening stage, Lagoa Azul, when local champion Joaquim Santos went off into the crowd. All of the drivers had been unnerved by the crowd's behaviour through the opening day and at the service the works crews held a meeting. By unanimous decision they threatened to go no further unless the rally organisers could guarantee better crowd control measures.

FISA's officials were incensed, as was Jean-Marie Balestre, who raised hell among the team principals, demanding that they call the drivers to heel and put them back in their cars. Lancia's team principal, Cesare Fiorio, was equally keen that the works cars – or at

least *his* works cars – should continue, but the drivers and co-drivers stood firm. In their view, the rally organisation was to blame for the fatalities in the crowd and they had no desire to see more injuries occur. Jean Todt endorsed his drivers' views completely.

All went quiet in Europe while the World Rally Championship teams headed for Kenya and the Safari Rally (where one more spectator was to be killed, this time by the Group A Volkswagen Golf GTI of Kenneth Eriksson after steering failure). When the WRC reconvened in Europe it was May and the Tour de Corse. Jean-Marie Balestre made sure that he was present for the occasion.

Before the start, the works drivers suggested some changes to the route to help reduce the risk to drivers and spectators. In response, the FIA president attempted to put the blame for the Portuguese disaster back upon the manufacturers, brandishing a letter, Macmillan-like, which he claimed had been signed by 58 drivers declaring the route to be safe and denouncing the manufacturers for building cars that were far beyond the levels of performance that he had intended for Group B.

Henri Toivonen had been laid low by 'flu in the days before the rally, but Lancia team boss Cesare Fiorio made sure that he was dosed up with medication and in the car for the start. Peugeot won the first two stages but then Toivonen took off into what appeared to be an unassailable lead – although he was far from happy.

'Honestly, now we have done more than

four hours stages', he said. 'First day: we have done more stage times than on [the] whole Rally of 1000 Lakes. I mean; this is really a mur[der] with these fast cars. We are having the acceleration from zero to 100 kilometres an hour: 2.9 seconds. From zero to 200 kilometres an hour: 9.6. I mean, those long stages that are 50 [kilometres] or more, there isn't the notes what's the crowd or what's the water, you know, it's unbelievable, you know. There's no brains which can work so hard.

'Well, everybody I have seen – they agree, and, well, at this moment they are really dead. I mean... this is crazy. This is crazy, even [if] everything is going very well but, I mean, if I have troubles I – I'm for sure completely finished.'

The second day of the rally featured two stages longer than 50 kilometres, the second of which was the 58.14-kilometre Campe Militaire Corte. Toivonen was fastest – as he had been all day – but then, after a short service halt, he went straight into the next stage, Corte-Taverna, from which neither he nor co-driver Sergio Cresto would emerge. As the ink-black pall from their burning car still hung over the hillside, Jean-Marie Balestre summoned a special council of his most senior officials to plan their response to the tragedy.

Balestre's position, when he presented it in

Rally HQ, was unequivocal. The Group B cars themselves, as created by the manufacturers, were to blame for the tragedies in Portugal and in Corsica. As a result, they would not be permitted to contest international events after 1 January 1987 and the plans for Group S would be abandoned entirely. From 1987 onwards, Group A production-based cars with a limit of 300bhp would be the senior class, with Group N 'showroom' models and Group B cars of less than 1,600cc engine capacity.

No investigation was carried out into the skeletal remains of Toivonen's Lancia, which were quickly spirited back to Italy; still less

ABOVE The last of the smoke hangs over the spot where Henri Toivonen and Sergio Cresto died on the Corte-Taverna stage; a terrible moment for rallying. *(McKlein)*

LEFT Jean-Marie Balestre immediately threw blame for Vatanen's accident (and that of Joaquin Santos in Portugal) at the feet of the manufacturers. *(McKlein)*

into whatever had been left of its crew. Neither was there anything other than a cursory look over the corner at which the crash took place, which revealed nothing – no tyre marks, no sign of the car having hit anything on the inside of the corner, no debris: nothing.

It would be two weeks before the manufacturers gathered in Paris at the BPICA to vote on whether they approved of Balestre's unilateral action to cancel their very expensive Group B programmes. Those who opposed Balestre's decision outnumbered his supporters by almost ten-to-one, and they went to the Place de la Concorde with this news in person.

Balestre's response to the dissent would be marshalled by his newly appointed head of the FISA Manufacturers' Commission: Max Mosley. The Englishman, son of Britain's fascist leader Sir Oswald Mosley, had a long history in the sport as a driver, as one of the founders of chassis constructor March and as the legal expert engaged by Bernie Ecclestone in his battles with Balestre over the commercial future of Formula 1.

Mosley had not been voted in to his role at FISA – he had secured only three votes, putting him a distant third – but Balestre ignored this aspect of the process and appointed him anyway. Mosley's job would be to try to convince the manufacturers to swallow the bitter pill of losing their investments in Group B, but he could see that the legal position of Balestre's announcement was

sketchy to say the least. The most obvious question for which the FIA had no answer was, if Group B cars were at fault, why were they not being banned immediately, rather than in January 1987?

Jean Boillot and Jean Todt tabled a motion to simply remove the turbochargers from Group B cars and run the existing cars with vastly reduced power output. Mosley and Balestre had no truck with the idea, stating that the FIA and FISA knew best when it came to safety, as the record of Formula 1 attested, where power outputs were growing year-on-year but deaths and injuries were becoming far less frequent.

That was on 13 May 1986. Two days later, during testing at Circuit Paul Ricard, Elio de Angelis crashed violently in Bernie Ecclestone's Brabham-BMW and was trapped in the burning wreckage, dying from smoke inhalation. The FIA's case in its argument with the BPICA looked tenuous indeed.

Then at the end of May, on the Rallye Hessen in Germany's national championship, another disaster befell Group B. Formula 1 driver Marc Surer was flying in a Ford RS200 while in pursuit of Peugeot's rally leader Michèle Mouton in her 205 Turbo 16. The car broke loose and skidded sideways into a tree, leaving Surer seriously injured and killing co-driver Michel Wyder in the resulting fireball.

Mosley, meanwhile, had been busily working on ways to get Balestre's ban on Group B secured. In the end, he decided that only those manufacturers competing in the World Rally Championship were eligible to take part in the final vote, and at a stroke the majority in favour of keeping Group B in some form disappeared: the result was 11 for and 11 against.

Emboldened by Mosley's success and having clearly seen that Peugeot was the biggest hurdle to a quick, clean death for Group B, Balestre let it be known in September 1986 that he was considering the removal of Peugeot's international competition licence as a manufacturer. Peugeot responded by suing the FIA for 300 million francs in compensation for the cancellation of Group B as a valid class.

At the Rallye Sanremo later that month, the Peugeot 205 Turbo 16s arrived with side skirts attached to the undertray of the cars, as they had been regularly since the Tour de Corse. The Italian officials passed the cars in scrutineering and Juha Kankkunen led the event until the scrutineers had a change of heart, immediately disqualifying the Peugeots for running an illegal aerodynamic device and refusing to let them finish the event under appeal.

It was widely assumed that this was just the Italian way of doing business. Victory for Lancia handed Cesare Fiorio's team the manufacturers' title and lead driver Markku Alén was duly named as drivers' champion, so it was suspected by many that the Italian authorities were simply backing the home team. However, it later emerged that the Peugeots' legality had only been questioned by the FISA delegate on site rather than the Italians, who were then duty bound to carry out the process of excluding the French team.

Peugeot put in a legal challenge to the treatment meted out on the event while the first preparation began of a new desert specification for the 205 Turbo 16. In the end, the results in Sanremo were declared void by

ABOVE The remains of Marc Surer's Ford RS200 on the Hessen Rally, in which the death of his co-driver Michel Wyder cemented the FIA's resolve to kill off Group B. (McKlein)

BELOW Andrea Zanussi's Peugeot 205 Turbo 16 shows the floor-mounted skirts declared by Peugeot to protect the fuel tanks from flying stones but adjudged to be illegal aerodynamic devices. (McKlein)

ABOVE The scale
of Peugeot's 1988
Paris–Dakar expedition
caused bewilderment
to Juha Kankkunen
and Juha Piironen, who
drove the leading 205
Turbo 16. (Peugeot)

Jean-Marie Balestre and the titles went instead to Jean Todt's team and its star driver of the season, Juha Kankkunen.

Peugeot had, meanwhile, been preparing to compete on the Paris–Dakar long-distance event, which began on New Year's Day 1987. As something of a free-for-all it was felt that Jean Todt's team would at least be safe from FIA interference... or so it seemed.

The French courts had been due to hear the 300 million franc case of Peugeot vs. the FIA in December 1986 but Jean-Marie Balestre was sidelined by heart surgery and the hearing was delayed until March 1987, when the court found in Peugeot's favour. The FIA immediately appealed and won its case the second time, although by then Group B was dead and buried and Jean Todt was fully occupied elsewhere.

In January 1988, Jean Todt's Peugeot team was back on the Paris–Dakar with a four-car 'maximum effort' consisting of two 205 Turbo 16s for Juha Kankkunen and Alain Ambrosino, with two 405 Turbo 16s for Ari Vatanen and Henri Pescarolo.

Kankkunen and Piironen had never known anything like the 13,000km (8,080-mile) trek before and several aspects caused them to blink a little. 'By the standards we have today, those cars were madness', said Piironen. 'Under our seats were 90 litres of gasoline and

behind our backs 300 litres more. In the front there was a tyre casted into a form and holding some 30–40 litres more.'

Vatanen led all the way to Bamako in Mali, where his car mysteriously disappeared, allegedly being held to ransom by a local criminal gang. Not everyone felt that the theft story held much water – among them, Juha Piironen.

'There are many stories about that incident', he said. 'I have been there and if you ask me, there will be a true story for that, but it is none of those which have been told. I really do not believe that the car was stolen. Something else must have happened. My personal opinion is that maybe the engine had been broken. The car had been then taken away somewhere where it is possible to change the engine in doggo. Then they have sealed it as it would be all okay. The service park mechanics are on their work, there is no chance to steal a car from service of one of the top teams. For a mechanic it would have been a natural act.'

The car was permitted to restart the event, even though it set off more than 30 minutes after its allotted time. By the rules of the event, Vatanen should have been excluded but a *force majeure* was declared and he was allowed to continue to the finish, where he should have been free to claim victory – were it not for Jean-Marie Balestre.

Having heard about the shenanigans with Vatanen's car, Balestre decreed that the organisers had no right to modify their own regulations during an event. In a heated exchange between Todt, the rally organisers and the FIA, Balestre allegedly called Todt the 'Napoleon of the Desert'. In reply, Todt told the French media that 'it is better to be a Napoleon of the Desert than the Bokassa of Motorsport.'

Nevertheless, Vatanen's exclusion from the results stood and the Peugeot 405 Turbo 16 would have to wait until another day to claim its first win. In the end it fell to Juha Kankkunen to notch up what was the last works victory of the Peugeot 205 Turbo 16. It marked the end of almost four years of continual work, preparation and execution of a remarkable project, and it made the Peugeot 205 one of the most iconic competition cars of all time.

'Our 205 story was much more than a car, it was really a human adventure', recalled Ari Vatanen.

'The fact that Peugeot, when they bought Talbot, it was the last thing they should have done. It really put Peugeot into big financial difficulties and when Monsieur Boillot, the president of Peugeot, decided: "Well, let's go into rallying and profit from this new generation of car", because Peugeot was

very conservative before the 205 was really becoming quite obsolete. But Monsieur Boillot was not supported by the Peugeot family or even the president of PSA. Yet he did it: they told him, Monsieur Boillot, you do it but it's at your own risk. And he gave free hands to Jean Todt to make it happen and within our team something very special took place. It was bigger than life.'

ABOVE In Dakar, both Ari Vatanen and Juha Kankkunen celebrated victory – although it would be Kankkunen and the Peugeot 205 Turbo 16 who were recorded as winners. *(McKlein)*

LEFT The story of the Peugeot Talbot Sport team was one of incredible successes, tactical brilliance and extreme engineering. *(McKlein)*

Chapter Six

The driver's view

The Peugeot 205 Turbo 16 was an analogue vehicle – it didn't even have power-assisted steering until well into its career. In the Group B era, drivers had to operate a heavyweight clutch – double declutching on downshifts – while left-foot braking and attempting to hold the car on something approaching its intended trajectory. And while doing all of this, they had to follow the guidance of their co-drivers while performing at ten-tenths.

OPPOSITE Ari Vatanen and Juha Kankkunen both led Peugeot Talbot Sport to incredible successes in the World Rally Championship and on the Paris–Dakar, masters of the art of taking the 205 Turbo 16 to the pinnacle of the sport. *(McKlein)*

On some events – particularly those in Latin countries – they also had to blot out the presence of a wall of humanity on either side of them, some of whom chose to run across the road in front of the oncoming cars, crouch on the apex of a corner to take photos or simply pretend to be toreadors.

The drivers did all of this while seated within a super-heated cell in which the combined noise of the engine, transmission, turbo, suspension and detritus thrown up by the wheels eclipsed that of the average heavy metal concert.

They did it for a week at a time, both day and night, over stages that could be 50 miles long. From our vantage point almost a quarter of the way through the next century it is utterly impossible to form a view on what that might have been like. Precious little in-car footage was ever filmed when Group B was in its pomp, and so our view of these cars being driven at ten-tenths remains as what little could be drawn from the fleeting glimpses of fearsome, noisy beasts flashing through the special stages.

As the online conversation rolls ever-onward in petrolheadland about which form of motor sport requires the most skill, or about why Group B deserves its cult status when modern cars achieve faster stage times, consider this: the magic might not be in the cars at all – but in the drivers.

BELOW Ari Vatanen won the 1984 RAC Rally after a consummate display throughout the opening days and a fightback after coming off the road on the penultimate night's running. *(McKlein)*

Think of it this way...

Top rally drivers today are still the most versatile talents in motor sport, who must be able to perform on all surfaces in all weathers. They still skitter on the ragged edge of adhesion and the trees, walls, street signs and houses that flash past can all exact the same toll now as they could then. But with modern suspension and modern tyres, with gearboxes that allow them to change gears like a PlayStation racer, it is like comparing someone writing and posting a letter with someone writing and posting a Tweet.

That is not to say that today's World Rally Championship drivers would have been out of their depth in the Group B era – far from it. But only a handful of drivers ever got to experience life at the wheel of a 500bhp, 900kg projectile designed from the ground upwards for the sole purpose of winning rallies, and only they are in a position to explain what that was like.

'My greatest, most pure pleasure was always to go as fast as possible around a corner', said Ari Vatanen.

'*Any* corner... the first corner, the middle corner – and the last corner. Even if you are leading by five minutes and it doesn't make sense to go anymore, I still too often had to go at the maximum for the pure pleasure of it. Everything else in my life has been the result of

that: braking late, get the tail out and just to go for it, for the pure pleasure of it.'

Competition drivers aren't generally known for their vivacity when it comes to describing their day jobs, but then that's one of the many reasons why Vatanen remains a hero beyond compare to rally aficionados around the world. When the 1981 world champion joined Peugeot, the 205 Turbo 16 was still very deep in the process of trial and error that marked its testing programme – and was a completely unknown quantity next to the traditional front-engine, rear-wheel-drive cars that Vatanen had driven to that point.

'The very first test in Italy was a disaster', Vatanen remembered. 'We were using a stage from the Sanremo and we broke lots of wishbones and things – it seemed to be one thing after another – but they fixed them very fast.'

Bearing the brunt of the testing programme throughout its development year was Jean-Pierre Nicolas: one of Jean Todt's trusted old friends on the team. Gruff and businesslike, Nicolas has always been most at ease behind the wheel, and his smoothness and consistency were a boon to the engineers when trying to find and rectify the prototype's many teething troubles.

Each of the five World Rally Championship victories that Nicolas had scored came on long, gruelling tests of a team's calibre. They came from being quick enough to challenge and smart enough to let the result come to him – maintaining the car, not leaving the road and building the all-important rhythm needed to get through the special stages. At Peugeot Talbot Sport, those virtues would be measured in the product he helped to create through the relentless testing schedule: the 205 Turbo 16.

'It is a privilege and you have to see it is above all a very interesting job to be able to collaborate with the engineers of the design offices of Peugeot for a whole season to do all the development of the car', Nicolas said. 'I find it extraordinary... it is very, very interesting work. An important, difficult mission.'

It was a difficult mission indeed, even for someone with Nicolas's breadth of experience. Nobody really believed that a mid-engined four-wheel-drive car could be built to run

effectively or reliably in rallying's top echelon – and when Peugeot did put the 205 Turbo 16 out into the real world for testing it was often wilful and invariably frail.

Learning which pieces would break and in what order, measuring how long they would last and how much reinforcement they needed was knowledge that the team built up rapidly through its intensive testing programme. Nicolas was the anchor for more than a year prior to the car's debut in the world championship, using his

ABOVE Jean-Pierre Nicolas (right) was a mainstay of French rallying in the 1970s, then became the defining driver who helped to steer development of the Peugeot 205 Turbo 16. *(McKlein)*

BELOW Jean-Pierre Nicolas's dedication to the team at Peugeot not only brought dividends to the 205 Turbo 16. After leaving the cockpit he joined the management and presided over three manufacturers' titles in the WRC with the 206. *(McKlein)*

Victory is always sweeter when it comes in the face of adversity, which is why the 1985 Monte Carlo Rally is remembered as the crowning achievement in Ari Vatanen's career. It was undoubtedly the most spellbinding performance that the brilliant Finn ever gave, but it is also an object lesson in the abilities of Jean Todt to identify and capitalise on every opportunity to achieve success.

The event could hardly have got off to a less auspicious start for Vatanen, whose pre-event recce was derailed by circumstances beyond his control. 'My very first co-driver with whom I drove, Martti Simonen, he died during the recce of Monte Carlo and of course I couldn't go to the funeral', he remembered. 'Then I was in the hospital during the recce, from Monday to Saturday, because I had bad back cramp like a knife in my back.'

An upset and ailing star, who had been forced to forego the essential pre-event practice to hone and refine the pace notes with co-driver Terry Harryman, was at quite some disadvantage when they rolled off the start ramp beneath the Eiffel Tower in Paris. Compared with the meticulous, regimented programme undertaken by Walter Röhrl and Audi, it hardly seemed likely that Vatanen's challenge would be up to much – and then on the second stage at St. Bonnet le Froid there was almost disaster.

'I ran into some spectators', Vatanen recalled. 'You know, I hit them and they go over the car! They go over the car and they broke the windscreen and they broke the radiator but luckily we had the service at the end of the stage.'

Throughout the early stages, Walter Röhrl sought to build an advantage. His Audi Sport Quattro was a wilful beast, nose-heavy and wildly over-powered, but Monte Carlo was rallying to Röhrl, and if he could not master it then he could no longer consider himself to be the best in the world. Such an outcome was unconscionable, so in one of the great performances of mind over matter, Röhrl won four of the first seven special stages to build a very healthy lead.

'I said to Terry Harryman at the end of Burzet: "Now this is guaranteed – Walter will win his fifth Monte Carlo"', Vatanen remembered. 'But then the following special stage I found a completely new... like I had got wings.'

Up until Burzet, the majority of the stages had been run on dry asphalt but increasingly the snow and ice of the Alpes Maritimes came into play. Unlike 1984, when there was unprecedented snowfall, or 1983, when there was very little, the 1985 event saw both road conditions come into play – often on the same stage. Jean Todt and his team went to work trying to keep Vatanen one step ahead of Mother Nature – giving him 'wings'.

Todt was forever receiving reports from the gravel crew up ahead, checking in with the remote service vehicles and dispatching helicopters to go and retrieve data on the road conditions. Where extra insight was needed, he was unafraid to call up stage marshals and officials for the latest view – after all, it was in no small part thanks to Todt and Peugeot that the 1985 Monte Carlo Rally happened at all, and one good turn deserved another.

Through the snowbound stages of St-Nazaire-le-Désert and St-Jean-en-Royans, the ideal setup of the Peugeot and the growing confidence of Vatanen saw him slash Röhrl's advantage to nothing and take the lead of the rally. For the next ten stages, Vatanen began to pull away to build a four-minute cushion until the field arrived at the Gap time control, where

BELOW An astounding performance at the wheel was backed by a brilliant team effort on the 1985 Monte Carlo Rally. (McKlein)

Terry Harryman managed to clock them in four minutes early and, under the rules, an eight-minute penalty was applied.

'I filled in a complaint in vain, and then calculated Ari's chances for the remainder of the rally', said Jean Todt. 'After considering the number of kilometres left, and the difference between Röhrl and Vatanen, I was certain that Ari was condemned to second place.'

Vatanen was anything but downcast, however. It was a setback, admittedly, but his faith in the car and the team was absolute. There were 16 stages remaining over the final 24 hours, and as he set off Vatanen said to Todt: 'We'll win anyhow.'

Over the next eight stages the four-minute deficit was reduced to 30 seconds. Dusk on the final night would bring the first run through the Col St. Raphael stage, where Todt's information was that there was snow and ice for the first 8km (five-mile) climb, but at the peak where the sun had been shining all day the road was dry asphalt for 22km (13.7 miles) to the finish.

'Röhrl drove past us fitted with racing tyres', said Todt, as the team agonised over their decision. In the end, Vatanen's car went out with narrow, studded snow tyres fitted and gambled on being able to make up enough time in the climb to be able to withstand the Audi's increased pace once the snow had cleared.

Such was Vatanen's advantage that he caught and passed Röhrl on the road within those first 8km and then skittered along at unabated speed on his narrow wheels as the dry asphalt tore the studs out. By the end of the stage he had a 90-second lead that would grow to more than five minutes by the time that the rally was over – without the penalty he was fully 13 minutes faster than Röhrl.

'It [the 205 Turbo 16] was inspiring, it gave real confidence, it was a psychological thing', Vatanen remembered. 'Maybe the engineers don't always realise that. Sometimes technically speaking maybe there is another solution. Their Excel table will give purely a better result if you do such-and-such but if it is not confidence-inspiring for the driver, you will not get wings.

'If the car is confidence-inspiring then it feeds itself – not always, but when it does like

ABOVE With his confidence sky-high in the car and his team, Vatanen gained 'wings' in the Alpes Maritimes, delivering arguably the greatest performance of his WRC career. *(McKlein)*

on that Monte Carlo Rally I exceeded myself because I was so confident that the car was so forgiving so even if I made a mistake the car would forgive me. So I was not afraid: you just go. You can almost close your eyes and you go and that's what Peugeot gave me, it's like my hand in a glove and it's part of me and I'm part of it. We are one entity.'

BELOW Completing the 34 special stages fully 13 minutes faster than Walter Röhrl's Audi, Vatanen and Harryman sealed a remarkable victory. *(McKlein)*

consistency to establish these baselines among the components.

So too was his consistency able to influence the development of the engine, transmission and chassis from a thunderbolt strapped to a bucking bronco towards that of a relatively user-friendly potential winner. These reference points were to test every last ounce of Nicolas's nerve, not least when he first ran at a competitive event at the testimonial for André Piot at Sarlat in the autumn of 1983, finishing second after a somewhat nervous time in one of the first gravel outings for the 205 Turbo 16.

'The route was just a single kilometre long, but the car kicked like a billygoat', Nicolas said. 'The programme was still in development – we had absolutely no spare parts. The smallest damage and we were out. The whole car was a prototype. The main issue was with the engine, the early one was not smooth enough. The operating rev band was only between 5,000–7,000 rpm. Impossible!'

The contribution that Nicolas made towards taming the prototype's wayward gravel handling cannot be overstated. As with any

French rally car it was natural that it should be a rocket ship on paved roads, but by diligently building experience on gravel, the team soon mastered such terrain sufficiently well prior to the car's early world championship adventures.

'What makes you win is the team', he remembered. 'It is of course the car, which means it is the whole team who wins and the brand because behind it all is the team... the quality of its engineers, its mechanics and drivers. You need to 'make mayonnaise' between the drivers, the engineers and the mechanics – and it's not easy.'

Sadly for Nicolas, however, his longed-for return to driving duties did not end with a fairy-tale sixth world championship rally victory to his name. He never truly expected that it would, but undoubtedly there was enormous satisfaction in being able to deliver that fine fourth place on the team's debut in Corsica – perhaps even in doing so when Vatanen had taken himself out of the running on the final day, although Nicolas is generous in his praise of the superstars of the sport.

'Drivers are like all great sportsmen: if they can do something well it is because they have character. Character with qualities and flaws and you need to channel it', he said.

'As a driver I have the great satisfaction to have been the driver who made all the tests – all the tests – of the 205 Turbo 16 because it was a great step forward in motorsport and in rallying.'

At the end of the 1984 season, Jean-Pierre Nicolas embarked on new adventures within Peugeot Talbot Sport, becoming the head of operations for the national rally programmes being run in Germany, Italy, Spain, France and Britain by the brand's various importers. This would be the first step on a journey to eventually succeeding Jean Todt at the head of an operation which he had been instrumental in building from the outset.

Stepping up to join Vatanen in 1985 would be the vastly experienced Timo Salonen. Without having either the physical vitality of Ari Vatanen or the resolution of Jean-Pierre Nicolas, Salonen was deeply discomfited by the 205 Turbo 16 on first acquaintance. The chain-smoking, rotund figure of Salonen was a natural talent, one whose innate feel for a car

BELOW Timo Salonen came to Peugeot as a suitable number two driver in support of Ari Vatanen – but ended up claiming the 1985 drivers' championship after a glorious winning streak. *(McKlein)*

meant that he was often seen driving with one hand on the wheel as though entirely at peace on a Sunday afternoon, rather than producing what were, without exception, the very fastest times that his outdated Nissan Silvia 240 RS could conjure up.

The Nissan was an extremely user-friendly car, light of steering and able to be placed with precision wherever the driver wanted it to be. The first evolution of the 205 Turbo 16 retained many of the prototype's skittish manners and it carried significant heft through the steering wheel, demanding greater physical effort from a driver who simply wasn't an Olympian in his approach to the sport. Adding even a fairly small degree of power assistance, however, transformed his performance overnight.

'We changed the steering for the Rally Portugal with a different steering rack and we made it a bit more responsive', Salonen said. 'In Portugal our speed was a little bit better – though the win came with the help of others having bad luck... but it came anyway.'

As ever, Salonen was modesty personified and the value of his win was in being there at the finish. It was certainly of value to Jean

Todt, who was fairly dismissive of Vatanen's performance on an event that has always been something of a car breaker:

'In the first stage, Vatanen had a flat', he later said. 'In the second, he made record time. Next stage, a joint snapped as a result of the earlier flat. The suspension collapsed. Ari, too impatient, ignored the signals from the mechanics in the helicopter surveying the car, to pull over for assistance. Finally, he raced into the service point much too fast, doing irreparable damage to the car.'

In contrast to his mercurial countryman, Todt's summation of Salonen's performance in Portugal was 'a stupendous job' and one which set a pattern for the rest of the season. Whether or not he was rattled by the speed that the oft-overlooked Salonen was carrying, there was a definite urgency in Vatanen's approach to 1985.

Those measured early stages followed by a decisive strike for victory that had characterised Vatanen's run of five victories for Peugeot had all-but faded into history. On each event, he was at ten-tenths from the start of the opening stage while Salonen, in his outwardly unhurried style,

ABOVE In Portugal, Salonen arrived with the car finally tailored better to his needs and duly claimed the first in a string of four victories in his title season.
(McKlein)

RIGHT Sitting alongside Salonen throughout his Peugeot career was long-standing co-driver Seppo Harjanne, the perfect foil. *(McKlein)*

was profiting from Vatanen's misfortune to build himself a championship advantage.

'We went to Greece to get a win and I had a feeling that the car is finally starting to keep in my hands and the speed is there', Salonen said. 'And that was a victory achieved by driving – we were in the lead from the beginning and it went nicely. Then we went to New Zealand to get a win and that was a tough one because none of the top drivers retired. We had to keep the speed up all the way to the end it was truly a win achieved by driving. We were happy for that, and we were planning a little summer vacation but our team principal Mr Todt had other ideas....'

Testing was an almost daily chore for the drivers throughout the season – although neither the swashbuckling hero Vatanen nor the laid-back Salonen particularly relished the prospect. Pounding through the many miles that were needed to keep the 205 Turbo 16 at the top of its game was one of the aspects of life that jarred with its big-name stars, and as a result a considerable burden fell upon Bruno Saby. As Salonen's co-driver, Seppo Harjanne, put it: 'Timo was more like an artist, rather than an engineer. He took the tasks with his laid-back manner, but did his job always well. There was not much work-out for him at that time... we did do some walking together, though.'

Argentina followed New Zealand, and with it came Vatanen's terrifying ordeal when he crashed out of the lead on the second special

stage and found himself hovering between life and death. The accident was caused by a known failing in the first evolution of the 205 Turbo 16 to behave itself over high-speed yumps, but for Salonen there was never a question mark about the car or in his commitment behind the wheel.

Speaking on Finnish TV after taking victory in Argentina, he explained how he was able to keep pressing home the team's advantage even after Vatanen's accident: 'The crashes are more vicious than they used to be', he concurred. 'Some years ago you could be a little crazy in a rally car. Not today, I don't dare anymore. I'm just trying to go as safely as possible. It's part of the job and I enjoy driving fast. The risk is there, which I take gladly because I enjoy the speed so much. And while driving I don't really think about the danger or anything like that.'

Jean Todt knew that he had the chance to win both the drivers' and manufacturers' titles at his first attempt if Salonen kept his form up and he could find a driver capable of stepping into a number two role that would allow both cars to reach the finish. One driver who had been setting the world on fire in Group A for Volkswagen, and who was dominating the German Rally Championship for Peugeot, was rising Swedish star Kalle Grundel and his time to shine would come with a call-up for the 1000 Lakes.

Jean Todt was insistent that there was no need for heroics on Grundel's part. With the new E2 variant of the 205 Turbo 16 at his disposal, Grundel simply had to finish in sixth place to seal the manufacturers' championship for Peugeot Talbot Sport – against a pair of two-wheel-drive Lancias and a pair of new be-winged Audi Sport Quattros, he could almost drive as he pleased. Thus when Grundel went off on the first stage of the rally, damaging his steering, Todt saw all that he needed to see of the Swede's suitability for a full-time drive.

'I was sad', Todt said of the event. 'I looked at Grundel while the car was being fixed. He was like a child caught in the middle of some wrongdoing; he must have been saying to himself, "I missed the chance of a lifetime." He was on the verge of tears.'

Eventually, Grundel managed to haul himself up to fifth place at the finish, just two seconds behind Henri Toivonen's Lancia – but the damage was done. Salonen took the victory and with it the drivers' title, while Peugeot Talbot Sport celebrated their manufacturers' crown and Grundel was largely left to himself, reflecting on what might have been.

As it became clear that Vatanen might never return to competition, so did Todt's efforts to sign a new star driver grow more urgent as the 1985 season drew to a close. He tested the water with both Walter Röhrl and Markku Alén once again, but neither wished to break with their existing manufacturers. Having taken one successful gamble on a lesser-known Finn, in the shape of Timo Salonen, Todt then decided to see if lightning could strike twice and called on Toyota's bright young star, Juha Kankkunen.

'It was a complete surprise!' Kankkunen remembered. 'I was in Ivory Coast; I'd won the rally. It was just after the rally and I got the call from Jean Todt from France: "Would you like to drive for Peugeot next year?" I had the contract already signed for two years with Toyota – or three years or something. And I said: "That's a question, sorry Jean, but you have to discuss with Ove [Toyota team boss Ove Andersson] on this or with that because I'm not the person that would like to do things like that".

'So then they had the long discussion and I flew direct from Ivory Coast to Paris. I had a first class ticket there and everything, a car

ABOVE Kalle Grundel was unstoppable in the German Rally Championship in his Peugeot 205 Turbo 16 – but his opportunity to step into the void left behind by Vatanen was lost. (McKlein)

waiting for me and then we went to Peugeot and then discussed about that and we made a deal!'

For Ove Andersson, losing Kankkunen must have been a considerable blow. He had made a big investment in the young Finn, who was clearly on a path to stardom after being tutored first by former Mini-Cooper and Ford Escort legend Timo Makinen, then was gaining knowledge and experience under the direction of Toyota's team leader Björn Waldegård.

BELOW Juha Kankkunen was a young protégé of hard-charging men like Timo Makinen and Björn Waldegård who won the 1985 Safari and Ivory Coast rallies for Toyota. (McKlein)

RIGHT Juha Piironen became co-driver for his old friend Juha Kankkunen in 1986, when they both arrived at Peugeot Talbot Sport and would remain together for several seasons. *(McKlein)*

BELOW Juha Kankkunen had the star power of Vatanen and was fast absolutely everywhere. The Peugeot 205 Turbo 16 proved to be ideal for his attacking style. *(McKlein)*

don't know – I just got on with it straight away', Kankkunen remembered. 'It was a well-balanced car and very easy to be quick. The only tricky thing was on the jumps. The rear of the Peugeot was kicking quite a lot, you know, at that time the suspension wasn't really good anyway, so you had to be careful on that. Compared to that, the Celica was like a fucking train, you know, going on the straight lines and things.'

Another thing that changed for Kankkunen was his co-driver, after working with Northern Irish stalwart Fred Gallagher throughout his days at Toyota, in no small part helping with his understanding and nuance in English. Previously, Gallagher had co-driven for another rising young Finn in the form of Henri Toivonen when they were at Opel and, before that, at Talbot – alongside Guy Fréquelin and Jean Todt.

Evidently some tension had occurred at this point, with the result that while Kankkunen transferred to Peugeot, Gallagher remained at Toyota. Thus a new pairing was established at Peugeot with Kankkunen being joined by garrulous Finnish co-driver Juha Piironen.

'In the past, Todt had fallen out with Fred Gallagher and was now with a discreet manner suggesting that it would be nice if Gallagher would not be the co-driver', Piironen said. 'Then Juha called me from Beijing and asked me to do the job.'

The two Finns had known one another for years, with Kankkunen having regularly slept on Piironen's floor back in Finland before earning a living from his craft. At Peugeot the pair enjoyed a curious working relationship because they elected not to use their mother tongue – Kankkunen preferring to hear the notes called out in English, thanks to his time spent alongside Gallagher.

'We tried to move back the notes in Finnish. But as it was our first rally together in a Group B car and the snowy mountains surrounded us, we had to rethink everything', Piironen said. It was a curious arrangement to many, but there was no doubting its effectiveness right from the start.

'First rally with Peugeot in Monte Carlo, before the turbo was blown, I was leading it – straight away!' Kankkunen chuckled, almost

Nevertheless, there was clearly little point in holding him back when Toyota was going to remain stuck with its two-wheel-drive Celicas for the foreseeable future, and no doubt Todt was offering sufficient compensation. So it was that at the start of the 1986 season, Kankkunen joined Salonen and the latest iteration of Jean Todt's superteam was created.

'It was a big step from the Toyota but I

35 years after the event. For Juha Piironen, the delays in getting the turbo repaired meant that desperate measures were needed to keep them from going out of the rally, leading to a seat-of-the-pants ride to the start of the next stage.

'We stalled the engine normally but it took really long for the mechanics to start it again', he said. 'I calculated rapidly that we had no chance to make it on time by driving through all the villages and small roads. Then I remembered a highway that was familiar to us already from recce. Juha floored the pedal and we drove at 200km/h [125mph] so that all the studs were flying away from the tyres and through the plastic body. There was something to see for people! We even had time to pass the two pay-stations and were just on time on a normal route and on our way to the next stage. It was a longer way to drive but much faster than the normal rally route we should have followed.'

Years later, Kankkunen allowed himself another chuckle at the memory of the sort of liberties that a driver could take on the road in the 1980s. 'On the Monte with the studs, yes, you could do a few tricks', he said.

'So maybe you go out and do the first stage, it's snowy, then the second stage you did it was dry. Usually there was a service in between every stage but I remember one was exactly like this; one right after the other. And the second stage was dry. So we do a little of that, 200km/h, a little bit sideways... and we did the second stage without studs, then. Simple as that!'

Kankkunen and Piironen would end their Peugeot debut in Monte Carlo with a fifth place finish, some six minutes ahead of the team's Monte specialist Bruno Saby. Next came the Swedish Rally, an event that required such a depth of specialist knowledge of snow driving that it took 30 years and four-wheel-drive for Hannu Mikkola to become the first non-Swedish winner of the event for Audi in 1981. Five years later, Kankkunen made his first-ever appearance in Sweden – and took an astounding victory.

That win was perhaps the last high point in Group B in its days of innocence. Sweden was all-too swiftly followed by the terrible string of tragedies that unfolded at the Rally Portugal, the Tour de Corse and the Hessen Rallye. Despite the heavy pall that hung over the sport, Kankkunen claimed back-to-back victories on the Acropolis and in New Zealand, then remained a top three finisher in every event to the end of the year, sealing his first

ABOVE Victory in Sweden at the first attempt was unheard of for foreign rally crews, but Kankkunen and Piironen revelled in the Peugeot's performance. *(McKlein)*

world championship title through consistency – albeit with a little help from the FIA's appeal process after the Sanremo exclusion was annulled (see Chapter 6).

For its drivers, the Peugeot 205 Turbo 16 was the ideal weapon. As Kankkunen explained to this author: 'There was no pressure with that car, if you do your job right you're either winning or be second. Salonen won the 1000 Lakes in '86 but it was close – 10 seconds or something like that. No real difference.

'The last day we was just cruising around because Jean Todt came on the last morning and said we had the lead of four minutes or something to the next car so, just, boys – drink your coffee and have a nice drive! An easy, simple meeting in the morning, just go and have a coffee and your cigarette or cigar and do your job like you know how to do it, just don't race each other!'

While Kankkunen and Salonen inhaled their breakfasts and led the charge towards the world championship in 1986, there were several other 'guest stars' in Peugeot's programme throughout the season. Opening the account in Monte Carlo was none other than former Audi star Michèle Mouton who, after a year largely spent on the sidelines at Ingolstadt, finally had her opportunity to

whip the adoring French fans into a frenzy by signing with Peugeot.

'The first impressions of the Turbo 16 are a more manoeuvrable car, they have more ... more normal I would say, compared to the Quattro, which is sharper, more nervous, longer', she said to the expectant French press immediately before the start of her debut.

'I have a little problem because I used to have a balance problem between the front and the back on the Quattro. The difference between front and back on the Peugeot is not so much and I battle a little bit on the snow but I hope it will come.'

In the end, Mouton's older-specification car gave out under her on the 14th stage in Monte Carlo, but the 1986 season brought a total of six wins from nine starts in the German Rally Championship, and with them the drivers' championship crown. Speaking to this author during the writing of the sister Haynes volume on the Audi Quattro rally cars, her opinion had changed little on the Peugeot 205 Turbo 16 from that formed on first acquaintance almost 35 years earlier:

'The handling of the Peugeot was quite different from the Quattro', she said. 'More compact, more nervous, agile, but kicking off from the back – but it was still a four-wheel-drive. So of course a little adaptation but the car was easier to drive and more fun!'

Another refugee from Audi also came to drive the car in its final WRC season, and in so doing fitted the missing link in the chain for Jean Todt. Back when the M24-Rallye project was still in its earliest design stages, Stig Blomqvist had been Talbot's new star driver and was intended to lead the programme to fruition right up to the moment when he jumped ship to Audi. Four years later, and with the 1984 drivers' title to his name, he finally climbed aboard the 205 Turbo 16 to make what would prove to be a pair of decisive appearances in New Zealand and Finland, scoring the points that would seal the team's second manufacturers' crown.

'It was lighter than the Audi', said Blomqvist. It was certainly quicker. But still I preferred the Audi for the 1000 Lakes: it did what I wanted so I could trust it. The Peugeot was a bit strange upon landing after a jump. All those

BELOW Michèle Mouton had been too famous for Jean Todt's selection process in 1984, but joined to win the German championship and contest a selected WRC programme. *(McKlein)*

cars with the engine in the back are bit funny like that.

'Today, I am sure, they could control that with better suspensions, but it was a problem back then. And it would have been better for the 205 if the engine had been rotating the other way – when you took off and lifted off the throttle, the gyroscopic effect made the car dip at the front. We tried adjusting the wing to make it better, but it always had that little dip.'

The Group B chapter of the World Rally Championship was closed with Juha Kankkunen belatedly being crowned in Paris. It may have been an ending of sorts, but just two weeks after the awards ceremony the Peugeot 205 Turbo 16s were once again on the starting line of a major international event: the 13,000km Paris–Dakar Rally Raid. And sitting in car number 205 was none other than Ari Vatanen.

When he crashed out of the lead on the 1985 Rally Argentina, thanks to that 'little dip' of which Blomqvist had spoken, the violence of the impact wrenched Vatanen's seat off its mountings and he was thrown around helplessly as the car rolled end-over-end for several hundred metres. He was pulled from the wreckage with fractured vertebrae, a smashed leg and smashed ribs – although darker days were yet to come.

'I had extreme – medically speaking – extreme lack of oxygen after the accident and again after the operation when my lungs stopped', Vatanen remembered. 'When my totally smashed knee was fixed in an eight-hour operation, the worst that the doctors were fearing was that I was full of liquid, like I was the Michelin man. But my lungs were not only punctured, I had eight ribs broken and two vertebrae and the very worst scenario happened when, after the operation, my lungs stopped working.

ABOVE A hiatus in Ford's Group B programme made Stig Blomqvist available to join the team for two events in 1986 – scoring vital points in the manufacturers' title. *(McKlein)*

LEFT The catastrophic injuries suffered by Vatanen in Argentina would lead to 18 months fighting both physical injuries and mental trauma. *(McKlein)*

'It all came very, very close to death. The oxygen level [in your blood] is nearly 97–98 normally and mine went down to 19–20, then 18. Normally you never come back from that anymore. It's *so* low – but somehow, miraculously, I came back from those low figures but then for several days I didn't awake from that. I was alive but not awake and there was a big doubt that maybe my brain was damaged because of the lack of oxygen. And then I awoke.'

Although Vatanen's body had come through the ordeal and was beginning to recuperate, the same could not be said for his mental state. As soon as he was stabilised, the fallen star was flown back to Paris to continue treatment for his physical injuries, but he was stricken with a profound depression and became obsessed with the idea that he had contracted AIDS from a blood transfusion in Argentina. Not only that, but also his irrational mind feared that he had somehow transmitted the virus to his beloved family.

Through 1986, Vatanen remained largely hidden away from the world, locked in with terrors over which there was no force that he could exert to clear them. He felt that doctors were conspiring against him, numbing himself with up to 20 milligrams of Valium per day and, as he described in his harrowing autobiography, his metabolism began to sink so low that he was in danger of dying simply because fear had eroded his will to live.

Salvation came through the sight and sound of rallying. After much cajoling, Vatanen was taken to see Timo Salonen, Juha Kankkunen and Stig Blomqvist finish 1-2-4 for Peugeot in the 1986 running of the 1000 Lakes and he had an epiphany.

'I awoke from this nightmare, which is a

nightmare multiplied by a million', Vatanen remembered. 'From then onwards my legs were not as good as they were before the accident. I was still in a weak state and limping and my legs were very, very weak but anyway a couple of weeks later I was already testing the rally car for the first time a little bit.'

One month after the 1000 Lakes, Ari Vatanen sat at the wheel of a Peugeot 205 Turbo 16 E2 on the start line of the Rallye Sanremo – taking the role of the zero car, making sure that the stages were clear before the competitive cars came out, and allowing Jean Todt the opportunity to see whether Vatanen could conceivably return to active duty.

'Even there I went off the road but luckily I was so sainted', Vatanen chuckled almost 35 years later. 'I had just sort of come out of my nightmare but we got away with that one!'

Fast forward another month, and Vatanen was in Africa alongside Shekhar Mehta and the team as they prepared Peugeot Talbot Sport for its first assault on the Paris–Dakar. Already, the long-wheelbase Peugeot 205 Turbo 16 was complete and their job was to plan the route, the service halts and to find the outer limits of the car's range and endurance to ensure that the event, which began on New Year's Day 1987, ran as smoothly as the Sahara might permit.

'The first testing in Dakar when we go in, it must have been in October–November, and we were in the most beautiful part of Africa', Vatanen recalled. 'And there we are out there on the plains, around a bonfire having meals, and we do this incredible test there in this breathtakingly beautiful scenery. And that is also completely unreal.'

The Paris–Dakar was still in its infancy as an event, very much remaining an amateur adventure in which a vast array of cars, trucks and motorcycles set off to try their luck in the desert. It was exactly the sort of event that could capture the collective imagination of France – and adding the trio of bright yellow Peugeots into the mix, under the eagle-eyed command of Jean Todt, was manna from heaven for the crowds waiting to see the field off on its way.

'So we start the rally and on the first special stage, and this is how life can be incredible

and I want to show what I have learnt', Vatanen remembered.

'It was only 6km [3.7 miles] long, the prologue just outside of Paris, and it was pissing down with rain, and there was an incredible number of people out there in the outskirts of Paris in this terrible weather, and I drive so slowly that Shekhar Mehta overtakes me. We were at half-minute intervals on this little stage but I let him go, and then the front end of the car collapses.

'I had not touched anything, the suspension just collapsed and there is this incredible photo where the right-hand front wheel is all up into the wing as if I had hit something but I had hit nothing. And there were people who were trying to hang on to the left rear end of the car trying to balance it for me by giving a contra-weight and there were people in the crowd who were saying: he must be nuts. There he

BELOW Remaining with Peugeot meant stepping out of the world championship to conquer new worlds when Vatanen returned to duty, starting with the Paris–Dakar. *(McKlein)*

is, he is barely alive and he has done 2km and the car is already smashed. And of course we were only 2km in and the car wouldn't turn.

'The special stage was in a quarry and so it had lots of hairpins to keep us in this quarry and I couldn't turn – I think I could only turn left. So all the hairpins in the quarry that turned right I had to go straight on, turn the steering wheel left and then reverse. So I went around the right-hand corners in this way – over them, turn left and reverse. And yet I was 279th so when we go to Africa everybody – every lorry, every van, every rally car – everybody was there in front of me. All of this was because the clip that holds the ball joint in the top suspension was faulty. That little clip had just gone, like it was not there.'

It took Vatanen some considerable effort to convince Jean Todt that he had not hit something, but the errant clips were replaced and he began to carve his way through the field when they reached North Africa, passing 120 other runners in the course of the first desert stage. He was often forced to take risks, diving off the clear route and risking the odds of finding hidden rocks or crevasses, but on this occasion fortune was with him. He duly made his return to victory and reached another summit in his recovery.

'We come to Dakar to win it and I tell you it was completely unrealistic, even thinking back on it now it was just unrealistic', he recalled. 'Coming back to life first, and then even after

that disaster start to finish the event was one thing, but to win it... unrealistic!'

Another very different challenge awaited Peugeot Talbot Sport after the celebrations in Dakar were over, with three more bright yellow 205 Turbo 16s heading off to a faraway country – in this case America, and the Pikes Peak International Hill Climb.

Once again, the same trio of drivers were lined up for Peugeot as had contested the Paris–Dakar: Ari Vatanen, Shekhar Mehta and Andrea Zanussi. The team arrived in the Rocky Mountains weeks in advance of the event, booking Pikes Peak exclusively to conduct an intensive test programme on its reconfigured 205 Turbo 16s: this time with the cars lightened by 140kg and powered by the latest

1.9-litre XU9T engine, pushing out something like 650bhp.

It was a maximum effort raid on an event that few in Europe had heard of before 1985, when Michèle Mouton had beaten the 'good ol' boys' of American motor sport and all their purpose-built V8 buggies and decades of experience using Audi's four-wheel-drive. Jean Todt wanted to take on his old adversaries from Ingolstadt one more time and wrest the Pikes Peak title from them as he had done in the World Rally Championship – but as the competition drew closer, so his star player was once again beset by doubts.

'I was struggling, really I mean struggling', Vatanen said. 'In all the testing that we did and all the official testing I was a lot slower

ABOVE Vatanen looked impressive every time he got behind the wheel at the great American hill climb, but was unable to match the pace of Röhrl's Audi Sport Quattro until changes were made. *(McKlein)*

ABOVE **Vatanen's desperation at being unable to match Walter Röhrl's times in practice at Pikes Peak forced Jean-Claude Vaucard (pictured with Vatanen) to take extreme measures.** *(McKlein)*

than Walter Röhrl. A *lot* slower. And I really felt because if my – if whatever little brain I may have – I am not sharp anymore.'

This was not a cheap exercise for the team to have undertaken – from kicking the power output up as high as it could be reliably made to go to taking over the little town and its giant hill for several weeks beforehand. Neither Mehta nor Zanussi were close to Vatanen in terms of time, but the team's star player was struggling under a cloud of self-doubt.

'So for the final night before the qualifying, the mechanics were all really tired and Jean-Claude [Vaucard] said: "No – let's add a second wing.' Just like that. And they were working all night and added the second wing on the back and no testing or nothing; just straight up on the start line on qualifying morning, and after three corners I realised: car is perfect. Car is transformed. I flew – after that I flew and instead of being for 10km 4–5 seconds slower, I was 3–4 seconds faster than Walter Röhrl.'

Without the modern digital read-outs or results available at the tap of a mobile phone screen, the moment when Vatanen realised the scale of the improvement was all the more dramatic.

'After 10km [6.2 miles] there's a restaurant on the left-hand side', he recalled. 'That's where the forest ends. That's where it was and the *Autosport* journalist at that time, Kevin Gormley, was there. He was with Walter, who had been in front of me. So all the times were there and then I came and I see that my time is... that *I* am... a lot faster than Walter. I was in tears. You have to put that, and put my life into context.

'It came from that accident, through unrealistic survival, then all the psychological problems and I had every reason to think that I am no more what I used to be. And there I am, with that time in front of me and you are so extremely grateful – you don't have to but of course if you believe in God you can thank God – but even if you don't believe in God you can thank life, what life has given to you.

'That grace is overwhelming, if you understand what I mean. You feel you are at the receiving end of something – there I realised as a driver that I was still there: I'm intact. I am still fast. It's incredible that feeling of how life is giving me so much, how God is giving me so much and I was in tears. And Kevin Gormley was the only journalist who was there at the finish line, and those are one of those frozen frames in my life – although I am lucky to have quite a few frozen frames in my life.'

Pikes Peak did not ultimately fall to Peugeot and Ari Vatanen in 1987 – although it was a near-run thing. In the end, a loose pipe cost the Finn his valediction and prevented Jean Todt from a clean sweep of winning every title that he had aimed for with the Peugeot 205 Turbo 16. The following year, Vatanen would indeed take victory at Pikes Peak, but it would come in the rebodied form of the Peugeot 405 T16, complete with four-wheel-steering and vastly different aerodynamics – and without the challenge of Audi or Röhrl.

For Vatanen and the mechanical parts of the 205 Turbo 16 there would be many more days in the sun that followed. He would win the Rallye des Pharaons in Egypt at the wheel of a Dakar-spec 205 before 1987 was at an end, and remain the anchor of Peugeot's Rally Raid squad until 1990 before transferring – along with the cars – over to PSA sister brand Citroën for a further seven years of success.

In the hands of Jean-Pierre Nicolas, the Peugeot 205 Turbo 16 evolved from an idea into a potentially all-conquering reality. Timo Salonen and Juha Kankkunen turned their other-worldly gifts towards delivering the world championship titles for which it was designed. Kalle Grundel and Michèle Mouton dominated competition in Peugeot's most important European market to humble both Audi and Ford on home ground, while the likes of Stig Blomqvist, Bruno Saby, Shekhar Mehta and Andrea Zanussi brought their specialist abilities to maximise the team's scores on gravel, asphalt and the African plains.

But the final word belongs to the man for whom the Peugeot 205 Turbo 16 brought a tumultuous 13-year story, consisting of the greatest highs and most terrifying lows that an athlete could ever experience. Across the world, this little French supercar is most closely associated with a man who took extraordinary victories in the world championship, conquered the Sahara and danced into the clouds. Ari Vatanen.

'It's like the violin. My father was a pianist and played the organ in the church – I don't play any instruments; about which I am sad because it is the most fantastic talent to be able to make music. Good music. This car, for me, was that. When you are a musician and you play to thousands of people at the Albert Hall or wherever – you're on your own. You just make the music. You close your eyes maybe but you don't miss the keys, you just make the music and you are in your bubble, and that is the feeling I know so well.'

BELOW With the addition of extreme new aerodynamic measures overnight, Vatanen's confidence was restored, completing a remarkable recovery from his physical and mental difficulties.
(Motorsport Images)

Chapter Seven

The owner's view

Buying and owning an historic competition car is a dream for many people. They represent heroism, design brilliance and performance on a level that not even the most rarefied strata of supercars can hope to emulate. A genuine ex-works Peugeot 205 Turbo 16 is nevertheless a car of astonishing rarity, comparable with cars like the Ferrari 250 GTO or ex-works Porsche 962 – although they still command only a fraction of the asking price.

OPPOSITE Owning a Peugeot 205 Turbo 16 is a rare privilege that will get you invited to some of the world's great motoring extravaganzas. *(Goodwood/Drew Gibson)*

Finding a unicorn

It is entirely understandable if the rarity, charisma and success of the Peugeot 205 Turbo 16 puts it near the top of a collector's wish list. Among rally fans around the world, the little Peugeot is usually third in any poll of favourites behind the mighty Audi Sport Quattro S1 and the evocative turbocharged-and-supercharged Lancia S4 – but neither of these contenders won the world championship. The Peugeot is therefore in a class of its own: a unicorn.

Buying a 205 Turbo 16 is a very expensive exercise and, as with any rally car, it is fraught with pitfalls. This is a model of which there were 200 road cars built to a specification that made them usable fast road cars, and then just 20 of each competition variant.

Mechanically, there was relatively little difference between the 197bhp road variant and the 350bhp first-generation rally car. Indeed, there was a bolt-on kit of parts available in period from Peugeot Talbot Sport that would allow upgrading to 300bhp with a roll cage for enthusiastic amateur drivers to go rallying.

This meant that in the decade immediately following the demise of Group B it was possible, with very little work, to construct a convincing replica very close to works specification. Then there is the question of how many cars were converted to long-wheelbase Raid specification, and how many more went off to compete in rallycross. There was very little sentiment shown in period for these cars, which had repaid their massive investment by 1986 but still had to earn their keep right through until 1990.

Establishing the full identity and provenance of any rally car is significantly more difficult than a comparable racing car. Everything on a rally car – even the bodyshell – is considered to be a consumable item. As can be seen in the table on pages 70–73, very often the works Peugeot 205 Turbo 16s would transfer number plates as one car was taken off active

duty and another car replaced it – making life particularly hard for historians and buyers alike.

'They always create a lot of interest whenever they come in to the auction, we always love having them', said John Poulson, auctioneer at Bonhams, which is one of the most obvious places for a collector to go when hunting for a prized rarity such as a Group B Peugeot. Bonhams keeps a very careful eye on which rare cars are where, how long they have been in any collection and how likely it is that a juicy morsel might be offered up for one of their hugely popular sales around the world.

'Things like Minis from the sixties, you're basically selling an identity because they would change the shell after every rally', Poulson continued.

'With Group B cars it's not as bad because it's within fairly recent memory, but I think that anyone buying one of these cars has to know that a particular shell may not have won the Sanremo Rally or whatever but it has a continuous history. That's what you're buying, that's the nature of rally cars and everyone accepts that.'

In leafy Surrey, independent dealer in racing, rally and high-performance cars Mark Donaldson grew up around Group B machinery because his father was a noted performer at the wheel of an MG Metro 6R4. An almost constant stream of Audi Quattros, Ford RS200s, Metro 6R4s and the occasional Peugeot has passed through his forecourt in recent years, bringing with them some unique insights into the market.

'I think you can be more confident with a Peugeot than with many cars because their internal records, if you're lucky enough to see them, are quite good', Donaldson said.

'The term of "ex-works" determines how a car left the factory rather than what happened during its tenure at the factory. So anything that is then changed, like a bodyshell, post-works, then that is the end of the coda, so it's no longer ex-works.

But if you're lucky enough to be able to attribute a specific bodyshell to a specific rally, or the rallies that it did, then you have a history... the hard thing is that unless you have that inherent understanding you're probably

LEFT Provenance is golden, as the owner of Bruno Saby's Tour de Corse-winning Peugeot would attest. (McKlein/ Slowly Sideways)

not going to buy one, quite frankly, because you have to have that pretty pragmatic understanding of it.'

This level of pragmatism when spending a significant amount of money requires a poker champion's nervous disposition – and expert guidance. Donaldson's suggestion that a car's specification is sealed at the factory of origin is shared by John Poulson. 'It is so difficult today to trace which car, or what proportion of which car, competed on a particular event but what you have to accept is the history and the continuous story of the car from being built to the moment that you buy it', the Bonhams expert explained.

BELOW Some rally cars became title-winning rallycross cars, making their provenance no less interesting or valuable. Here the car campaigned by Matti Alamäki leaps through Goodwood's Forest Rally Stage. (Goodwood)

Assuming that you have this sort of expert guidance to call upon in order to navigate the choppy waters of identifying an historic rally car's provenance, the next question is most likely to be which car to buy. For most potential buyers, the choice lies squarely between the early competition 205 Turbo 16, a study in simplicity and redolent of Ari Vatanen's days in the sun through 1984–85, or the later be-winged and lightened E2 variant, the car that won back-to-back world championships.

It is the later cars that have a higher value and are altogether more sought-after for their rarity as much as anything. Mark Donaldson stated: 'A lot of the Evo 2s got converted into Raid cars and so about five proper Evo 2 rally cars remain as they were. Most of them had the wheelbase extended, extra fuel cells put in them and went to the desert.

'I think one of the original Evo 2s with a lesser history changed hands for just under a million euros recently – certainly within the last three years. I think that same car, which was an increment or two above anyone's perception, would go for the same value in a nanosecond.'

With only five genuine cars to choose from, perhaps it would therefore be simpler to avoid

RALLYING IN MINIATURE

It is entirely understandable if £500,000 is more than most enthusiasts have available to spend on a collectors' car. Even if this is a remarkably small amount of money for a world championship-wining piece of technology with bags of charisma, there are limits, after all.

So how does an enthusiast get their hands on something special to show their passion for Group B's champion of champions? Usually, they head for a model shop.

There are a host of diecast models in various scales to grace a shelf or a desk, or if that isn't sufficiently hands-on then there are plenty of model kits to choose from. But rally cars were created with action in mind, and you get plenty of that on a slot rally.

Slot racing (better known as Scalextric

ABOVE Scalextric's little Peugeot 205 Turbo 16 negotiates a miniature Monte Carlo Rally stage – a regular slot rally sight. (*Author*)

RIGHT Combining slot racing action with railway modelling attention to detail, slot rally stages can be works of art as well as torturous to master.

(*Phil Field*)

the costlier E2s and revert back to the earlier specification of 205 Turbo 16s, with their KKK turbos and less-sophisticated electronics. Not so, say the experts.

'Collectors want the best or nothing', Mark Donaldson said. 'So although Evo 1s are great cars they will not get close to the Evo 2s for desirability or value.

in Britain, or Carrerabahn in Germany) puts an electric motor into a model (usually 1/32 scale) and lets the driver control how much power that motor receives as they navigate the track. Usually these are two-lane sets laid out on the carpet at home or four-lane layouts at a slot racing club. But not all.

It was rally-mad Spain that decided to take slot racing and turn it into a timed event consisting of special stages. These would be built up to eight at a time by event organisers, with one car running at a time against the clock. Drivers would circulate in groups just like a golf foursome, each marking the other's timesheets as they moved from one stage to the next.

In many cases, the construction of stages has now become as elaborate and detailed as a model railway layout. Monte Carlo, Sweden and the Dakar can all be made in miniature, with inclines, tunnels, jumps and hairpins. Some even have a water splash (ionised water prevents fusing the local area), while surfaces can be realistically given a dusting of snow (icing sugar) or mud (cocoa powder).

In recent years, Scalextric has produced a very fine scale Peugeot 205 Turbo 16 in the later E2 format. It is more of a toy than an outright competition car but it is proportionally and anatomically quite correct, and can offer a lot of fun for minimal outlay.

If full-blooded competition is on the agenda, however, there is only one place to go: the Slot Racing Company in Spain, which now produces a Peugeot 205 Turbo 16 originally

designed by Original Slot Car. With a range of torquey motors, several different tyre designs and compounds, and suspension on all four wheels with varying strength or springs, these cars have dominated their class in slot rallying for several years.

Slot rallying has become a mainstay of the hobby, not only in Spain but also across most of continental Europe, Britain, Australia and North America. In the 2010s, Slot Rally GB was a ten-round national championship that ventured from Wales to Norfolk and from Lancashire to Hampshire – in which the OSC Peugeots were an almost-insuperable force.

It may not be exactly the same as hurtling through a stretch of forest at ten-tenths, but as a sociable day out for all ages it takes quite some beating.

BELOW These two OSC Peugeots have been treated to a service barge and mechanics, showing how complete slot rally prep needs to be. *(Author)*

is something of a challenge, and in this characteristic the Peugeot is no exception. The four-wheel-drive system is considerably more advanced than, say, an early competition Audi Quattro, but it still graunches and groans, and the car still understeers at low speed and drivers get plenty a fulsome work-out thanks to what are, by most standards, fantastically heavy controls.

Jostling for prominence with the transmission whine and the road rumble is, of course, the throaty XU8T engine sat just behind the passenger's kidneys, which seems at times to exist simply to feed the whistling, snorting turbo. None of this is especially sonorous in the same way as a road-legal Ferrari, Jaguar or BMW competition car, which rather limits opportunities to take it down to the pub.

Road sections were only ever a means to an end: the chance to move from one timed special stage to another. It is really only at full tilt that the experience of driving a Group B car makes sense, ideally on a stage where four-wheel-drive traction makes the world hurtle past at certifiable speed. For many years there were few opportunities to let these cars stretch their legs – but now, at long last, they do so at numerous major events across Europe.

Rallying with a Group B

At the end of 1986, Group B cars of more than 1,600cc were no longer permitted to compete on FIA-sanctioned rallies. This meant that the cars either fell dormant or they were modified for different types of competition – Audi and Peugeot tackling Pikes Peak, Peugeot heading for the Sahara, while all manner of Group B cars from Audi, Peugeot, Ford, Lancia and Austin Rover were sold off to privateer entrants for use as rallycross cars – prompting the first great wave of enthusiasm for the discipline around the world.

Often the specification was changed considerably for what would prove to be long years of much harder use than these cars had ever seen on special stages. If any rallycross cars had started with a works rally history, by the time they had done a couple of seasons of biffing and bashing around the European rallycross calendar there would be very few original components left unscathed.

ABOVE The definitive title-winning 'E2' version of the Peugeot 205 Turbo 16 commands a hefty premium – but only five genuine examples are believed to exist. *(Goodwood/ Drew Gibson)*

BELOW Historic rally events for Group B cars have found a following through the Internet, where period footage shows how spectacular these cars were to new generations. *(McKlein/ Slowly Sideways)*

'Hypothetically, I'd say that there's a high point of around €1.2 million for an Evo 2. With the Evo 1s, there are a few more of them and they're still great cars. From personal experience, I sold one with a good history that went for around £500,000. That's a very repeatable figure for the earlier cars.'

The price tag of £500,000 to £1,000,000 seems absurdly small when compared with many other cars of similar rarity that achieved much less. However, the value of a Peugeot 205 Turbo 16 is always going to be limited by a number of factors, such as how user-friendly it is to take out on the road, whether it is a pleasant place for the owner to put their friends or paramours for a Sunday afternoon drive and what sort of events your ownership will get you invited to.

Driving any Group B car on the road

They did not stop rallying, however. In Britain, the MG Metro 6R4 was permitted to run in 'Clubman' specification on national events, provided that the engine was not producing more than 300bhp. In South Africa, meanwhile, the national importer for Audi continued its unbroken run of success in national championships with full-house Audi Sport Quattro S1s boasting almost 600bhp until 1988.

Having slipped largely from view, however, Group B took on a somewhat mythical status among car enthusiasts – the 'Killer Bs' that were 'so fast they had to be banned'. The rise of the Internet revived old footage of Audi Quattros and Peugeot 205 Turbo 16s, which became readily and freely available to a growing number of people. Before long, there was considerable demand to see these cars back in action.

Tim Foster runs the group Rallying with Group B, which holds demonstration events for these cars, primarily in the UK. Foster grew up around these iconic cars and was determined to find the means for them to make a public return.

'For a long time there was nowhere that we could run the cars, because MSA were quite within their rights not to upset the FIA and refused to allow us to run them', he recalled. 'Yet the passion to run them was always there. There was no set structure from insurance purposes to even allow demonstration runs, so it's taken a lot of years and it's taken a lot of chipping away at the MSA and getting their support to allow us to run.'

Rallying with Group B is now the anchor group at events such as Race Retro, which takes place each February at the National Agricultural Exhibition Centre at Stoneleigh in Warwickshire. This event opens the classic and historic season in Britain, and for most visitors it is the rally action out on the site's paths and roads that makes the biggest draw.

'It's surreal, really!' Foster said. 'So many times, people will come out with cars that you never thought that you would see again. You've got to make it worth people's while obviously, the events have to be of a standard in terms of their organisation and the route needs to be good.

'Owners can do 50 stage miles this weekend over the three days if they wish. There are some full-scale events that can't actually offer competitors 50 miles these days, so I think that helps draw the sort of entry that we are fortunate to see.'

ABOVE Group B cars tend to perform demonstrations rather than compete on timed stages. That does not mean that the drivers aren't pressing on or comparing times. *(McKlein/Slowly Sideways)*

BELOW Huge crowds gather at the major European events to see stars and cars from the past going through their paces. *(McKlein/ Slowly Sideways)*

and John Davenport, the former head of Austin Rover's competition department, have built a rally Mecca at which crowds can see the best historic rally cars in Europe being put through their paces and usually a number of campaign veterans such as Stig Blomqvist and Timo Salonen are on hand to meet the fans and drive the cars.

'The Eifel Rallye Festival is a demonstration event for historic rally cars which does not have any kind of timekeeping', said Slowly Sideways spokesperson Norbert Kettenhofen.

'However, the event is run on closed rally stages previously used in the German Rally Championship and the drivers will certainly not be cruising slowly round them.... The reason that the Eifel Rallye Festival is a demonstration event is that we like to present a wide range of historic rally cars – and this includes the Group B supercars that are not allowed to take part in any kind of normal rally.'

Group B cars do run against the clock at another event, Rallylegend, which takes place in San Marino each September. This is far from a 'normal rally', however – purely for the ebullience with which most of the owners tend to tackle the asphalt stages, to considerable good cheer from the throng lining the two special stages of the event.

Mark Donaldson has sold cars that have gone on to be given outings at both of these events and witnessed the rebirth of Group B

ABOVE It's not only the cars that are drawn to the best historic events, but also the drivers. Here, Stig Blomqvist and Timo Salonen take a turn at the autograph desk, while both regularly also take a turn at the wheel. *(McKlein/ Slowly Sideways)*

Entries to the right sort of events also add a significant premium to the value of a classic competition car, and in this respect Group B cars have enjoyed a golden era in recent years. Doyen of rally photography, including providing most of the images for this book, is Reinhard Klein. His unique ability to capture not only the cars but also the landscapes and culture of each event spanned the entire Group B era, for which his passion helped found the 'Slowly Sideways' movement.

The jewel in the crown of Slowly Sideways has become the Eifel Rallye Festival, which is held in Daun near Aachen each July. Klein

RIGHT Being 'Goodwood eligible' adds a significant premium to a historic competition car, and the Peugeots are always popular. *(Goodwood/Jochen van Cauwenberge)*

as a historic category. 'There's a lot of smaller events as well', he said. 'But for me, I don't think that any has yet got the perfect combination of the cars being what the show is built around – and some owners want to feel that *they're* the ones that people have come to see.

'Comparing historic rally events to the Le Mans Classic is really interesting because that event has such a peak in terms of entries and spectators. If Le Mans held that event annually, though, I think it would lose its appeal. At most historic events, spectator numbers have dropped to the point where the spectators aren't spectators in the traditional sense, they're just competitors who aren't out in that particular race.'

Bonhams auctioneer John Poulson also believes that the right event is what really puts values on an upward path. 'If there was a way of coming up with the ultimate Group B event with a seriously good special stage that was located somewhere really glamorous then the values will obviously be affected', he said.

'The nature and quality of the events really do have an effect on the value of the cars because, yes, they're a lovely thing to own but if there's a reason to own one and somewhere that you want to go to use it then it adds a significant premium.'

The most glamorous venue for British enthusiasts to seek out historic motor sport is Goodwood. Here, the circuit racing fraternity is catered to year-round at the Members' Meeting and Revival on the historic motor circuit, while Goodwood House itself plays host to the annual Festival of Speed. Each year, the Festival of Speed sees rally cars of all eras, including Group B, go through their paces on the Forest Rally Stage – a gravel-tracked run through the trees at the top of the hill climb route, which was laid out under advice from none other than 1983 world champion, Hannu Mikkola.

'If something's Goodwood eligible you can write your own ticket to some extent – or you can start building it, arguably!' laughed Mark Donaldson.

'Probably the ideal is to build an authentic "tool-room" replica, use it and enjoy it while always being open that the genuine car with provenance is at home. You're using and enjoying the car as it was meant to be, in its natural environment, recreating those iconic performances – while at home you've got the actual car that took part in those classic events and it's not getting worn out or damaged.'

Rising values have proven to be a new and difficult obstacle for event organisers to contend with. Although Rallying with Group B still produces entry lists with up to 180 cars for events like Race Retro, organiser Tim Foster has come to accept that a number of the cars may not have unblemished histories.

'As event organisers we have to be honest with ourselves and say, look, this is a dying breed. Is the replica movement something that we want to be involved in or not?' Foster

ABOVE A lot of owners prefer running on paved surfaces to spare their priceless paintwork. *(McKlein/Slowly Sideways)*

said. 'I don't think that there's a right or a wrong answer, really, but obviously holding FIA paperwork is some sort of endorsement of what the car is and what the paying spectator is ultimately going to see.'

Juha's crown jewel

Out of all the Peugeot 205 Turbo 16s in the world, whether in museums or in collections, there is one car that stands head and shoulders above them all. Not the least reason for that is that it has only had one (relatively) careful owner from new: 1986 World Champion, Juha Kankkunen.

Even while he was driving, Kankkunen set about collecting the key cars from his career – into which category one particular car had to be included. With chassis number C208, this is the car in which he achieved the hitherto unthinkable of being the first foreign driver to take victory in Sweden on his first visit to the rally.

'That's the car I've got', chuckled Kankkunen. 'Swedish winner car... it's straight from the factory to me and like brand new,

basically, and the idea is that it's not restored. It's cleaned, it's serviced and things but it's not like most of them – it's original.'

Kankkunen has built one of the greatest rally collections in the world – largely consisting of cars that he drove in his storied career on the way to winning four world championship titles. 'It started as a crazy idea in 1992', he said. 'I wanted something physical that my family could enjoy from my career. Carlos [Sainz] has a car and Didier [Auriol] has a couple, but I wanted to go further....'

Not only does Kankkunen hold original cars that he drove, including Toyotas, the Peugeot and a bevy of Lancia Delta Integrales, but he also owns some key rivals. He has a Ford RS200, an MG Metro 6R4, a Lancia Delta S4 and Audi Sport Quattro S1 that he bought from Hannu Mikkola.

The man entrusted with the care of these cars, including the most precious of all the surviving Peugeots, is renowned preparation expert Kari Mäkelä. His company, MAT, builds and maintains both modern and historic cars, with Group B as a particular speciality. It is from

BELOW Arguably the most important Peugeot 205 Turbo 16 in existence is C208, owned by the man who drove it to victory on the 1986 Swedish Rally, Juha Kankkunen.
(Kari Mäkelä)

MAT that the majority of rally-prepared Ferrari 308 GTS cars have appeared in recent years, while Mäkelä restored his own piece of history in the form of an ex-Mikkola Audi Quattro A1, which took more than a decade to complete.

Compared with his Quattro project, tending to Juha Kankkunen's Peugeot 205 is a much more straightforward proposition for Mäkelä. 'You can't really break much; it's strong and well-made and, if you have a Peugeot with history, you want to keep it original', he said.

'You don't do the rough stages; you do tarmac rallies mainly. You drive it carefully. It's a funny car, because normally if you have to change the cam belt it's a big job, you have to take it all apart to get to it. But this Peugeot, even the driver and co-driver can do it because it's just there. The little panel behind the co-driver door, you pull it out, you have the spare belt and then you go again. You just turn it so the marks are in the right place and then go.'

Today, Kankkunen's cars only turn a wheel rarely, but when they do it is at an appropriate speed... for a four-time champion, that is. Most often he is found giving ice driving masterclasses or touring the world's great events – but he still has time to roll out one of his former steeds from time to time, and never holds back.

'You never really lose the speed', he said. 'It's all about motivation. Are you still willing to risk everything? If you're not fighting, there's no point being.'

Fortunately, Kankkunen can afford to enjoy himself in the Peugeot because it is so robust. Kari Mäkelä is a great admirer of the robust, engineer-friendly concept behind the 205 Turbo 16.

'It's funny because the modern cars, if you break the belt, that's pretty much it', he said. 'Certainly for the rally, but maybe destroy the whole engine. It was in quite a dangerous place, the belt, right there in front of the rear wheel. Always you have small stones flying around there and just a little plastic cover over the whole thing – but it works.'

Just like everything else about the Peugeot 205 Turbo 16, even maintaining one is elegant in its simplicity. It's a design that not only proved devastating in terms of its performance, but also remarkably well thought-out. A true champion in engineering terms.

ABOVE Kari Mäkelä looks after all of Juha Kankkunen's museum fleet, plus his other customers and his own projects at the MAT workshop.
(Kari Mäkelä)

BELOW Owning and enjoying a Peugeot 205 Turbo 16 needn't be mechanically taxing and should prove highly rewarding to any collector.
(McKlein/Slowly Sideways)

Appendices

Appendix 1: Championships won by the Peugeot 205 Turbo 16

1985	FIA World Rally Championship for Makes
	FIA World Rally Championship for Drivers – Timo Salonen / Seppo Harjanne
	German Rally Championship – Kalle Grundel / Peter Diekmann
1986	FIA World Rally Championship for Makes
	FIA World Rally Championship for Drivers – Juha Kankkunen / Juha Piironen
	German Rally Championship – Michèle Mouton / Terry Harryman
1987	Paris–Algers–Dakar – Ari Vatanen / Bernard Giroux
	Rallye des Pharaons – Ari Vatanen / Bruno Berglund
	FIA European Rallycross Championship Division 2 – Seppo Niittymäki
1988	Paris–Algers–Dakar – Juha Kankkunen / Juha Piironen
	FIA European Rallycross Championship Division 2 – Matti Alamäki
	French Rallycross Championship – Guy Fréquelin
1989	FIA European Rallycross Championship Division 2 – Matti Alamäki
	French Rallycross Championship – Philippe Wambergue
1990	1e Trophée Andros – Eric Arpin
	FIA European Rallycross Championship Division 2 – Matti Alamäki
	French Rallycross Championship – Jean-Manuel Beuzelin

Appendix 2: Production of Peugeot 205 Turbo 16

1984	200 Peugeot 205 T16 road cars for homologation
	20 Peugeot 205 T16 E2 rally cars
1985	20 Peugeot 205 T16 E2 rally cars
1986	5 x Peugeot 205 T16 Grand Raid (converted from existing 205 T16 E2 stocks)
	3 x Peugeot 205 T16 Pikes Peak (converted from existing 205 T16 E2 stocks)
1987	2 x Peugeot 205 T16 Grand Raid (converted from existing 205 T16 E2 stocks)

Appendix 3: Descendants of Peugeot 205 Turbo 16

Peugeot 405 T16 Grand Raid	1988–90	Extended 205 Turbo 16 chassis, XU9T engine, transmission and running gear
Peugeot 405 T16 Pikes Peak	1988	
Citroën ZX Rally Raid	1990–97	
Peugeot 905 Spider	1992–94	XU engine architecture carried over
Peugeot 405 Mi16 Touring Car	1992–95	
Peugeot 306 Maxi	1995–98	
Peugeot 406 Touring Car	1996–2000	
Citroën Xsara Kit Car	1998–2002	
Peugeot 206 WRC	1999–2004	
Citroën Xsara WRC	2002–06	
Peugeot 307 WRC	2004–05	

Appendix 4: Rally Raid victories by the rebodied Peugeot 205 Turbo 16

1988	Rallye des Pharaons	Ari Vatanen / Bruno Berglund	Peugeot 405 T16 Grand Raid
	Baja Aragōn	Ari Vatanen / Bruno Berglund	Peugeot 405 T16 Grand Raid
	Pikes Peak International Hill Climb	Ari Vatanen	Peugeot 405 T16 Pikes Peak
1989	Paris–Tripoli–Dakar	Ari Vatanen / Bruno Berglund	Peugeot 405 T16 Grand Raid
	Rallye des Pharaons	Ari Vatanen / Bruno Berglund	Peugeot 405 T16 Grand Raid
	Baja Aragōn	Jacky Ickx / Christian Tarin	Peugeot 405 T16 Grand Raid
1990	Paris–Tripoli–Dakar	Ari Vatanen / Bruno Berglund	Peugeot 405 T16 Grand Raid
	Rallye des Pharaons	Ari Vatanen / Bruno Berglund	Citroën ZX Rally Raid
	Baja Aragōn	Ari Vatanen / Bruno Berglund	Citroën ZX Rally Raid
1991	Paris–Tripoli–Dakar	Ari Vatanen / Bruno Berglund	Citroën ZX Rally Raid
	Rallye des Pharaons	Ari Vatanen / Bruno Berglund	Citroën ZX Rally Raid
1992	Rallye des Pharaons	Pierre Lartigue / Michel Périn	Citroën ZX Rally Raid
	Rallye Tunisie	Pierre Lartigue / Michel Périn	Citroën ZX Rally Raid
	Paris–Moscow–Beijing	Pierre Lartigue / Michel Périn	Citroën ZX Rally Raid
1993	Rallye des Pharaons	Timo Salonen / Fred Gallagher	Citroën ZX Rally Raid
	Baja Aragōn	Pierre Lartigue / Michel Périn	Citroën ZX Rally Raid
	Baja 1000 Portugal	Pierre Lartigue / Michel Périn	Citroën ZX Rally Raid
1994	Paris–Dakar–Paris	Pierre Lartigue / Michel Périn	Citroën ZX Rally Raid
	Baja Aragōn	Timo Salonen / Fred Gallagher	Citroën ZX Rally Raid
	Rallye Tunisie	Pierre Lartigue / Michel Périn	Citroën ZX Rally Raid
	Baja 1000 Portugal	Pierre Lartigue / Michel Périn	Citroën ZX Rally Raid
	Atlas Rally	Pierre Lartigue / Michel Périn	Citroën ZX Rally Raid
	Baja Italia	Pierre Lartigue / Michel Périn	Citroën ZX Rally Raid
	Montée d'Olympe	Pierre Lartigue / Michel Périn	Citroën ZX Rally Raid
1995	Grenade–Dakar	Pierre Lartigue / Michel Périn	Citroën ZX Rally Raid
	Baja Aragōn	Pierre Lartigue / Michel Périn	Citroën ZX Rally Raid
	Baja Portugal	Ari Vatanen / Fabrizia Pons	Citroën ZX Rally Raid
	Atlas Rally	Ari Vatanen / Fabrizia Pons	Citroën ZX Rally Raid
	Baja Italia	Pierre Lartigue / Michel Périn	Citroën ZX Rally Raid
	Montée d'Olympe	Ari Vatanen / Fabrizia Pons	Citroën ZX Rally Raid
1996	Grenade–Dakar	Pierre Lartigue / Michel Périn	Citroën ZX Rally Raid
	Baja Aragōn	Ari Vatanen / Gilles Picard	Citroën ZX Rally Raid
	Baja Portugal	Pierre Lartigue / Michel Périn	Citroën ZX Rally Raid
	Rallye Tunisie	Pierre Lartigue / Michel Périn	Citroën ZX Rally Raid
	Baja Italia	Pierre Lartigue / Michel Périn	Citroën ZX Rally Raid
	Montée d'Olympe	Pierre Lartigue / Michel Périn	Citroën ZX Rally Raid
	Paris–Oulan–Batour	Ari Vatanen / Gilles Picard	Citroën ZX Rally Raid
	Baja España	Ari Vatanen / Gilles Picard	Citroën ZX Rally Raid
1997	Baja Aragōn	Pierre Lartigue / Michel Périn	Citroën ZX Rally Raid
	Baja Portugal	Ari Vatanen / Gilles Picard	Citroën ZX Rally Raid
	Rallye Tunisie	Pierre Lartigue / Michel Périn	Citroën ZX Rally Raid
	Paris–Samarkand–Moscow	Ari Vatanen / Gilles Picard	Citroën ZX Rally Raid
	UAE Desert Challenge	Ari Vatanen / Gilles Picard	Citroën ZX Rally Raid

1993	Pierre Lartigue / Michel Périn	Citroën ZX Rally Raid
1994	Pierre Lartigue / Michel Périn	Citroën ZX Rally Raid
1995	Pierre Lartigue / Michel Périn	Citroën ZX Rally Raid
1996	Pierre Lartigue / Michel Périn	Citroën ZX Rally Raid
1997	Ari Vatanen / Fred Gallagher	Citroën ZX Rally Raid

Appendix 6: Where to see Peugeot 205 Turbo 16s today

Type	Name	Location	Website
Event	Eifel Rallye Festival	Germany	www.eifel-rallye-festival.de
Event	Vosges Rallye Festival	France	www.vosges-rallye-festival.com
Event	Race Retro	UK	www.raceretro.com
Event	Goodwood Festival of Speed	UK	www.goodwood.com
Event	Castle Combe Rallyday	UK	www.castlecombecircuit.co.uk
Event	Rallylegend	Italy	www.rallylegend.com
Museum	Coventry Transport Museum	UK	www.transport-museum.com
Museum	L'Aventure Peugeot	France	www.laventurepeugeotcitroends.fr
Museum	Loheac Manoir de l'Automobile	France	www.manoir-automobile.fr
Organiser	Slowly Sideways	UK/Germany	www.slowlysideways.de
Organiser	Rallying with Group B	UK	www.rallyingwithgroupb.net

Appendix 7: Peugeot Talbot Sport – core team, 1982–90

Jean Todt	Director, Peugeot Talbot Sport
Olivier Quesnel	Manager, Peugeot Talbot Sport
Avila Ravier	Personal Assistant to M. Todt
Des O'Dell	Technical Director (1981–82)
Jean-Claude Vaucard	Technical Director
André de Cortanze	Chief Designer
Bernard Perron	Chief Project Engineer
Jacques Levacher	Design Manager
Philippe Jarry	Engine Manager
Patrice Cailloton	Design Engineer
Dominique Gérard	Design Engineer
Jean-Pierre Boudy	Powertrain Manager
Guy Andouse	Assistant Powertrain Manager
Jean-Pierre Hulin	Transmission Manager
André Massy	Suspension Engineer
Jean-Pierre Vitre	Production Manager
Marcel Vieublé	Competition Manager
Charley Pasquier	Co-driver/Logistics Manager
Carlos Barros	Chief Mechanic
Jean-Pierre Colinot	Team Engineer
Guy Andouse	Engine Manager
Jean-Pierre Nicolas	Test Driver/Promotional Manager
Jean Happe	Marketing Manager
Corrado Provera	PR Director
Jean-Claude Lefebvre	PR Manager
Jean-François Bouzanquet	Press Officer
Jacquelin Klien	Press Officer
Danièle Trevisanello	Finance Manager
Jeff Davis	Graphic Designer

Appendix 8: Buying and restoring Peugeot 205 Turbo 16s

Type	Name	Location	Website
Auctioneer	RM Sothebys	Global	www.rmsothebys.com
Auctioneer	Bonhams	Global	www.bonhams.com
Auctioneer	Artcurial	France	www.artcurial.com
Dealer	Mark Donaldson Sports & Competition Cars	UK	www.markdonaldson.com
Dealer	FA Automobile	France	www.fa-automobile.com
Preparation	Geoff Page Racing	UK	www.geoffpageracing.com
Preparation	Mäkelä Auto Tuning (MAT)	Finland	www.mat.fi

Index